Alongside the Person in Pain

Alongside the Person in Pain

HOLISTIC CARE AND NURSING PRACTICE

Morva Fordham SRN SCM RNT BScPsych MSc PhD

Formerly Lecturer,
Department of Nursing Studies
King's College, University of London
London, UK

Virginia Dunn RN BSc Nurs MSc Nurs

Fellow and Macmillan Clinical
Lecturer in Nursing
National Institute for Nursing
Oxford, UK

Baillière Tindall

LONDON   PHILADELPHIA   TORONTO
SYDNEY   TOKYO

Baillière Tindall   24–28 Oval Road
_____   London NW1 7DX, UK
W.B. Saunders

The Curtis Center
Independence Square West
Philadelphia, PA 19106–3399, USA

Harcourt Brace & Company
55 Horner Avenue
Toronto, Ontario M8Z 4X6, Canada

Harcourt Brace & Company, Australia
30–52 Smidmore Street
Marrickville, NSW 2204, Australia

Harcourt Brace & Company Japan
Ichibancho Central Building
22–1 Ichibancho
Chiyoda-ku, Tokyo 102, Japan

A catalogue record for this book is available from the British Library

ISBN 0–7020–1452–4

This book is printed on acid-free paper

Typeset by Phoenix Photosetting, Chatham, Kent
Printed and bound in Great Britain by Mackays of Chatham PLC, Chatham, Kent

Contents

Foreword

This book is written at a time when available knowledge about pain is growing rapidly. New findings about likely mechanisms involved in persistent pain open up exciting possibilities for developing new methods of pain control. Over time, this information may help us to better understand and even treat some types of pain. However, whether we always completely understand what is going on or not, we need to help people who have pain in the best way we can. The importance of keeping the individual who has the pain upper most in our minds as we try to provide sensitive, flexible care has not diminished, and is the central theme of this book. There is a welcome emphasis on what it means to have pain and a range of perspectives are encompassed. The book grapples with the philosophical aspects of pain, as well as more practical approaches as to what can be done about it.

We all want to provide the best possible care we can for people in pain. If this is to be achieved, what 'best possible care' really means cannot remain abstract, but needs to be clearly defined. We need to look systematically at what helps and what hinders the process of providing good pain management, both as individuals and as a team. Efforts to plan how good pain management can best be achieved are given added urgency by the current political emphasis on providing good quality care of known effectiveness. Research over several decades suggests that health professionals have often fallen short of such an achievement in many areas of pain management. This timely book really grasps the nettle and offers many opportunities to benefit those people we care for who are in pain.

Being alongside the patient in pain is fundamental to this book. It implies accessibility without imposition. Such a partnership involves all the partners contributing their own perspective, and perhaps expecting to work hard to get such a partnership right. The partners' backgrounds and traditions, each often seen as 'the right way', may be quite different. A respect for the unique contribution of each person in the partnership is crucial to its success. Health professionals can act as a resource in areas where the patient may have little knowledge (for example, appropriate analgesics or other methods of pain control), just as the patient can act as a resource in areas where the health professional may have little knowledge (such as the patient's expectations of pain and pain relief). Thus resources are pooled to the benefit of all.

How patients perceive their pain is important, and this is bound to differ between patients. This is of vital importance because people with pain do not exist in a vacuum; they have their own individual backgrounds. Their experience will be influenced by this background, and if we fail to take it into account, our understanding and ability to help will necessarily be impaired. If you are not alongside the person with pain, you run the risk of managing their pain out of context, working to perhaps different and not necessarily compatible goals. It is important to recognize how each of us views pain, as well as how the person with the pain (and others significant to him or her) view it. The identification of any conflicts between these views and use of negotiation for their resolution is essential. This book recognizes the potential personal costs of being alongside people in pain, and the need for the nurse not only to support and enable, but to be supported and enabled is acknowledged.

When I first started being interested in pain management, I felt poor pain management was inexcusable, and the goal of pain management should always be complete pain relief. Over time, I have somewhat slowly realised that good pain management is a complex and subtle art. I still feel a lack of any systematic attempt to manage pain is inexcusable, but my blind, almost evangelical adherence to complete pain relief has been modified. Complete pain relief may well be achievable, appropriate and what the person in pain wants. However, you need to know that. I have begun to realise that pain management which is acceptable to the person with pain, achieved via negotiation, is closer to the mark. This covers a whole range of activities, at times straightforward, at times incredibly complex. Exactly what is involved and the amount of negotiation that is appropriate or necessary can depend on many things. These include the type of pain, the person with the pain, and their own beliefs about the pain and its management. If I had been able to read this book when I started, my gradual recognition that what I thought was right was not necessarily how people with pain would see things, then I might have been able to provide more sensitive and effective care much sooner.

The authors have addressed a complex and diverse area in a sensitive and thoughtful way. I think this book will help those working with people in pain to understand their own beliefs about pain, the beliefs of those in pain and to use this and other related knowledge and skills to come alongside the person in pain in an accessible and responsive way. This will reap dividends when they plan and evaluate care, and facilitate the achievement of the best possible care for people who are in pain.

Kate Seers BSc PhD RGN
Senior Research Fellow
National Institute for Nursing
Radcliffe Infirmary, Oxford, UK

Preface

The contents of this book reflect the authors' attempt to explore the nature of the relationship between people who have pain and those who care for them. If this relationship is to be therapeutic we need to understand what it is to be in pain and what it is to be a carer.

Nursing is at the interface of conventional medicine, complementary therapies and common sense and so requires some understanding of the implications of knowledge in many fields, including physiology, medicine, psychology, sociology, philosophy and religion. We have tried to introduce these strands of knowledge.

We acknowledge our indebtedness to those nurses who have clearly and persistently focussed professional attention upon the problem of patient pain, and dedicated themselves to the promotion of compassionate, creative and competent care.

Our views have been shaped by our families and friends, by practitioner, teacher and researcher colleagues, by those we have taught, those who have cared for us when in pain and most of all by the people in pain we have nursed. We thank them all. We specifically thank Melissa Clough and Lisa Manley who contributed nursing care studies describing the care they gave when students; and clinical nursing specialists Ali Jesson and Jenny Jones who shared insights into their role in cardiac and orthopaedic care respectively.

We also wish to thank the publishers for giving us the opportunity to write this book and especially Sarah James for her encouragement and patience. We accept full responsibility for our failure to learn and understand as well as for any errors in the text.

Morva Fordham
Virginia Dunn

1

People and Pain

And a woman spoke, saying, Tell us of Pain.
And he said;
Your pain is the breaking of the shell that encloses your understanding.
Even as the stone of the fruit must break, that its heart may stand in the
sun, so must you know pain.

From *The Prophet*, by Kahlil Gibran

This book is about some of the problems faced by people in pain and considers some of the issues that they and their carers have to resolve. It attempts to address some questions about what it means to be in pain and what is implied by being a nurse or carer. What do nurses bring to the relationship that could be or is helpful and therapeutic? Hopefully readers will not passively accept the views expressed, but will actively agree or disagree, challenge and search for the best ways of knowing and being.

The authors' concern is with caring for people who have pain, whether or not the cause of their pain is understood. However, it does focus upon the consideration of physical and psychological problems rather than psychiatric problems (see Merskey, 1967; Tyrer, 1992). Using Copp's subdivisions of pain (Copp, 1985) we include:

1. Pain associated with disease.
2. Pain caused by therapy.
3. Pain caused by nursing care.
4. Pain associated with the patient's decision to forgo treatment.

Pain associated with disease includes acute and chronic, tractable and intractable pain. Therapy-initiated pain includes transient pain incurred by some investigations and physical treatments, as well as the consequence of invasive surgical procedures. Most pain due to therapy is foreseeable and temporary; occasionally it is unpredictable and can be more intractable than the original pain (Jensen and Rasmussen, 1989). Pain caused by nursing care includes any pain that is provoked or exacerbated by attempts to achieve activities of daily living with or for the patient. Pain associated with the patient's decision to forgo treatment includes pain endured by those who do not wish to use pharmacological or non-pharmacological remedies for pain, or pain developed as a result of untreated pathology.

The understanding of pain also necessitates some discussion of research-initiated pain, and the overarching category of life pain (Copp, 1985). Research-initiated pain is mostly experienced by healthy volunteers or animals rather than by the sick. Patients with pain may be involved in research into alternative methods of pain relief which succeed or fail to varying degrees in overcoming their pain. Such research only occasionally involves the initiation of pain. Life pain or the suffering associated with being human is pain from which no one escapes.

The choice of the title *Alongside the Person in Pain* is an attempt to reflect the nature of the relationship of nurses with patients, embracing the concept of caring as being with or alongside the person in pain; trying to see pain from the sufferers' perspective, including their meaning, their goals, their chosen interventions and their outcomes.

THE PHENOMENON OF PAIN

Humans have attempted from time immemorial to make sense of the experience of pain, to understand what it is, why it occurs and what makes it go away. The experience of pain is intimately related to the processes of life: birth, development, growth, learning, giving birth, work and dying. Some people experience pain more frequently and more deeply than others, but every society, each generation and all individuals at some time grapple with the phenomenon of pain. Many of the ideas that patients and nurses have about pain have existed for a long time and have been the focus of religious or philosophical thought and writing. Whether recent increases in understanding of the anatomical and physiological basis of the pain experience have had any impact on or relevance to the meaning of pain to individual sufferers is debatable. Some people seek and welcome scientific information, others do not. However, theories such as that of 'gate control' have undoubtedly had an immense impact on the understanding of pain phenomena (Melzack, 1990).

Merskey (1980) discussed the history of the idea of pain. Two problems recur throughout the ages: firstly, the overlap and confusion between the concepts of pain and suffering; secondly, the mind–body dichotomy, typified by views of pain as an emotional experience (Plato) versus the view of pain as a sensation resulting from damage to the body.

PAIN AND SUFFERING

We all have some experience of pain and so know to some extent what pain is. It is a sensation, an emotion, a physical state and a mental state. It can be considered to be evil, unpleasant, terrible, frightening, to be avoided at all costs—or good, easily forgotten, temporary, worth risking, a useful experience. Pain makes insistent demands on those who have it to take up some attitude towards it. Paradoxically, although pain is considered a negative phenomenon, the outcome can be positive (see the discussion of the meaning of pain in Chapter 3). Some people in certain circumstances or cultures may view pain as an honour, as a challenge, as a refining fire, as ennobling. Other people (or the same people in other circumstances) view pain as punishment, deserved and to be endured.

Lipowski (1970) attempted to categorize the meaning of illness to the sick person, and Copp (1974) found that patients described pain in ways that could be similarly categorized. Some patients regarded their pain as a challenge, as something to fight and overcome. Some felt it was a sign of personal weakness, whilst others perceived pain as a deserved punishment. Pain was also recognized as an opportunity to be creative, to learn about oneself and to increase understanding of and empathy with others.

The word 'pain' is not precise in its meaning and is used to cover a whole gamut of experience. C. S. Lewis (1940) made the following distinction between the term used in a narrow or trivial sense and the term used to embrace the concept of suffering of all types. Pain in the narrow or trivial sense (sense A) he described as:

> A particular kind of sensation . . . recognised by the patient as that kind of sensation, whether he dislikes it or not (e.g. the faint aches in my limbs would be recognised as an ache even if I didn't object to it).

The wider concept of pain (sense B) Lewis described as:

> Any experience, whether physical or mental, which the patient dislikes. It will be noticed that all pains in sense A become pains in sense B if they are raised above a very low level of intensity, but that pains in the B sense need not be pains in the A sense. Pain in the B sense in fact, is synonymous with 'suffering', 'anguish', 'tribulation', 'adversity' or 'trouble' . . . .

Lewis's 'problem of pain' arose from his desire to reconcile the apparent incompatibility of belief in a God who is good, loving and all-powerful and yet allows us to suffer pain.

When Copp (1974) interviewed 148 people in hospital, she began by thinking that she was studying pain, but concluded that she was actually being told about suffering, using the word 'suffering' to connote 'the state of anguish of one who bears pain, injury or loss'. Copp (1985) in her consideration of six aspects of pain, denoted something similar to Lewis's B pain as *life pain*, suggesting that 'we might appreciate that some aspects of life pain (separation, loss, grief, loneliness, anxiety, stress, etc.) are present in any potential patient. Even before disease, he is not then, without pain'.

In a thoughtful and thought-provoking article by Cassel (1982) entitled 'The nature of suffering and the goals of medicine', the relationship of suffering to organic illness and treatment was discussed. Suffering (taken to be the effects of illness, drugs, surgery, radiotherapy, etc. upon the person as a whole) was defined as:

> The state of severe distress associated with events that threaten the intactness of the person. . . . Suffering can occur in relation to any aspect of the person, whether it is in the realm of social roles, group identification, the relationship with self, body or family, or the relations with a transpersonal, transcendent source of meaning.

Cassel summarized the relationship of pain and suffering as follows:

> People in pain frequently report suffering from the pain *when they feel out of control, when the pain is overwhelming, when the source of the pain is unknown, when the meaning of the pain is dire or when the pain is chronic.* [Authors italics] In all these situations persons perceived pain as a threat to their continued existence—not merely to their lives, but to their integrity as persons. That this is the relation of pain to suffering is strongly suggested by the fact that suffering can be relieved, in the presence of continued pain, by making the source of the pain known, changing its meaning, and demonstrating that it can be controlled and that an end is in sight. (For further discussion, see Cassel, 1991.)

Part of what these writers seem to be saying is that pain is always felt in a total context of suffering; that the patient is whole—even if the health care is not holistic. We never experience pain in some 'pure' way, but always in the context of our psychosocial milieu. Pain is experienced in the context of our society, religious beliefs, family and work environment, our personal past experience and our current circumstances. Our understanding and interpretation of other people's pain are influenced by the same factors.

Pain is not, however, always accompanied by suffering, as is beautifully illustrated by an idiosyncratic view of menstrual pain given by Anne Frank (1954), aged 14 years and 6 months:

> I think that what is happening to me is so wonderful, and not only what can be seen on my body, but all that is taking place inside. I never discuss myself or any of these things with anybody: that is why I have to talk to myself about them. Each time I have a period—and that has only been three times—I have the feeling that in spite of the pain, unpleasantness and nastiness, I have a sweet secret, and that is why, although it is nothing but a nuisance to me in a way, I always long for the time that I shall feel that secret within me again.

So pain and joy can occur together when the cause of the pain is welcomed and the pain itself is not overwhelming. This paradox is probably less rare than is generally acknowledged. Physically and emotionally intense experiences as in sporting exertions can be accompanied by pain and joy at the same time or sequentially. The 'high' of the athlete has been reported and may be attributed to the release of endorphins (naturally produced opiates). The pain of labour is followed by the joy of delivery. It should be noted that not everyone will experience both positive and negative aspects, but pain is not always accompanied by or experienced as a state of anguish.

BODY AND MIND

Pain is an experience of the whole individual—mind and body. It may arise from peripheral pain-provoking stimuli (nociceptive pain), from within the nervous system (neurogenic pain) or have an emotional or psychological origin (psychogenic pain). Nociceptive and neurogenic pain have an organic basis; psychogenic pain has a psychological or mental basis. These conventional distinctions (Diamond and Coniam, 1992) seem clear enough but in fact can be a source of confusion and even cruelty instead of care. When 'in the mind' is regarded as synonymous with unreal, made-up or imaginary pain, carers may feel justified in ignoring the symptom and may even label the person as a liar or malingerer. As McCaffery and Beebe (1989) stated:

> All pain is real, regardless of its cause. Almost all pain has both physical and psychological components. . . . 'Pure' psychogenic pain may be defined as a localized sensation of pain caused solely by mental events, with no physical findings to initiate or sustain the pain.

Explanations afforded by Western science and medicine have made it easier and more respectable for us (and many of our patients) to believe that physical traumas can result in mental and emotional responses, than to believe that mental states can result in physically perceived symptoms.

The mind–body problem is evident in the difficulty of defining pain. Melzack, in his preface to *The Puzzle of Pain* (Melzack, 1973), stated the central dilemma clearly:

> Pain is such a common experience that we rarely pause to define it in ordinary conversation. Yet no one who has worked on the problem of pain has ever been able to give it a definition which is satisfactory to all his colleagues.

Degenaar (1979), a philosopher, when discussing pain, stated:

> I thought I knew what pain was until I was asked to say what the word 'pain' means. Then as is usual in such cases, I realised my ignorance. However, I do not think this is an isolated experience, it applies to many everyday words and no person who tries to define such words escapes the sobering effect of this basic human ignorance.

Sternbach (1970) suggested that pain is an abstract unifying concept that we use as a label for many different 'kinds of things' or phenomena. In an earlier book (Sternbach, 1968) he suggested nine descriptions, the choice of which was dependent upon professional usage and education—i.e. pain is an elementary sensation, a complex perception, an emotion or affect, a neurophysiological activity, a neurochemical stress reaction, reflex adaptive behaviour, the result of internal psychic conflicts, interpersonal manipulation, and the human condition. Degenaar (1979) expressed a similar point when he wrote:

> Neurologists speak in terms of nerve impulses, psychologists in terms of emotional qualities, philosophers in terms of sensations, feeling, suffering and meaning, and theologians in terms of guilt and punishment.

Degenaar (1979) helped to clarify the task of understanding the phenomenon of pain by suggesting that we conventionally use three kinds of descriptions of human reality corresponding with 'body language', 'mind language', and 'person language'. By 'body' he means the physical and physiological dimension of the human individual, by 'mind' the experiencing and conscious dimension, and by 'person' the meaning-giving and social dimension (Table 1). Nurses have to understand all three languages and make some synthesis of their own understanding in order to interpret and integrate both patient experience and medical knowledge.

Table 1   Descriptions of human reality

Terminology	Human dimensions
Body language	Physical and physiological
Mind language	Experiencing and conscious
Person language	Meaning-giving and social

From Degenaar (1979).

PUZZLES AND PARADOXES

Many aspects of the phenomenon of pain are difficult to understand, and make McCaffery's working definition of pain, that it is 'whatever the experiencing person says it is and exists whenever he says it does' (McCaffery, 1972), central to the nursing assessment and care of patients in pain. Recognition that there is no clear, predictable, unequivocal relationship between injury and pain is puzzling, and has been a major spur to furthering our understanding. Why do some (rare) individuals not feel pain at all? Why do we sometimes feel pain without any apparent cause? How can limbs continue to hurt after they have been removed? Why is some pain felt as excruciating when the cause seems so trivial, yet some major injuries give rise to no pain at all, at least for a while? Why do we sometimes hurt all over, and sometimes only in very localized places? Why is pain sometimes felt far away from the site of disease, and sometimes precisely and solely at the site of injury? The paradoxical nature of our experience of pain may add to our puzzlement. For example, sometimes pain and pleasure seem to be poles apart—at opposite ends of a continuum—whilst at other times pain and pleasure seem to be inextricably and closely connected. On the one hand, the experience of pain is vital for survival, for making us pay attention to damage and learning to behave safely. On the other hand, the experience of some intense, unrelieved pain is associated with sustained shock and eventual death. Is pain a foe or a friend? Is pain an enemy or an ally? Can it be both at the same time?

There are also paradoxes concerning the response to pain. The manifest and unjustified failure of nurses and other health carers to recognize the unnecessary and often severe pain suffered by the physically ill (Seers, 1987, 1989) has led to the current almost messianic call to relieve or prevent pain. No surgical patient should be in pain (Royal College of Surgeons of England, College of Anaesthetists, 1990). Pain relief has been described as the core of nursing practice (Sofaer, 1983). *Stop all pain now* is the new message.

However, if we honestly consider how humans spontaneously respond to pain, in some cases paradoxically the response is to enhance the pain and experience it to the full. Many a painful tooth is pushed, pulled and waggled by the owner and the enhanced pain evaluated before pain relief is sought. Muscle cramp pain in foot or leg is stamped and walked upon. The use (arguably abuse) of the limb is instinctively recognized as the quickest method of obtaining relief despite the initial increase in pain. People with one pain may resort to the self-infliction of others pains (and injuries). Paradoxically the semiwild activity and the secondary pains may reduce the experience of the first pain to bearable proportions. White clenched fists, nails dug into palms and bitten lips are regular responses to the anticipation and endurance of other pains. The hands and arms of nurses not infrequently become surrogate pain bearers during brief painful procedures.

PREVALENCE AND INCIDENCE OF PAIN

Prevalence is the number of cases in existence at a certain time usually in a specified area or country. *Incidence* expresses the rate at which a certain event occurs, as the number of new cases of pain occurring during a certain period.

If we take the definition of pain as that of life pain, then the experience is 100%; likewise, if we take the definition of pain as any experience however trivial or minor, then again with rare exceptions (Melzack, 1973) the experience will be 100%. There have been many pain prevalence studies as well as estimations made by those whose main life work has been with patients in pain. Bonica (1982) speculated on the basis of epidemiological studies and his own wide experience that 'nearly a third of the people of industrialised countries have chronic pain and of these, half to two thirds are either partially or totally disabled for periods of days, weeks, months and sometimes permanently.'

The prevalence of pain in Great Britain was estimated as approximately 5 million in 1990 (Rigge, 1990). A Swedish study of the prevalence of pain in a general population was undertaken by Brattberg *et al* (1989). From a sample of 827 respondents ranging in age from 18 years to 84 years they found that when asked about 'any pain or discomfort', 66% reported that they had pain during the past 6 months; 15–20% reported pain in neck, shoulders, arms, lower back and legs which affected them 'to quite a high degree'. Pain was most frequently reported in the age group 45–64 years, being found in over 50% of both men and women. Typically, pains in the musculoskeletal system were described as being continuous and of lower intensity compared with head and face pains which were intermittent but of higher intensity.

A study of the incidence of pain in a population of 454 adult medical and surgical inpatients in the USA was reported by Donovan *et al* (1987); 353 of these patients (79%) experienced pain during hospitalization, and 58% of the 353 experienced excruciating pain at some stage of their admission. Other studies have attempted to estimate the incidence of pain and distress in particular groups of patients according to diagnosis or age. For instance, there have been many studies of labour pain, which according to Bonica (1984) and Melzack (1984) explode the myth of painless childbirth. Melzack *et al* (1984) found that among primiparae pain was reported as extremely severe by about 25% and as severe by a further 38%. Multiparae had lower pain scores, but even so 46% rated their pain as severe or extremely severe. The pain of women who received preparatory childbirth training was statistically significantly lower than the pain in those who had not received such preparation, but levels were high none the less.

Increasingly invasive investigations and surgery are undertaken on day patients. Their early discharge means that untoward symptoms including pain are difficult to monitor. A study of sterilization by tubal ligation by Fraser *et al* (1989) investigated the pain of 54 such women and found that 85% reported pain (and/or fatigue) during the first 4–5 days at home sufficient to delay the resumption of normal activities.

Attempts to estimate the experience of pain at either end of the lifespan are faced with difficulties of choosing valid assessment criteria. In children the problem is partly one of interpreting non-verbal responses, and in the elderly reluctance to report pain is sometimes evident. However, Craig *et al* (1984) began their article on the developmental change in infant pain expression with the statement that 'Pain has no boundaries with respect to age'. Studies of pain in childhood have led to the conclusion that the most common recurrent pains in childhood are abdominal pain, occurring in 10–15% of children, limb pain in 15% and head pain in 15–20% (Schechter, 1984). Abu-Saad (1984) suggested that paradoxically the incidence of pain in children may be increasing as survival and treatment of chronic and life-threatening disease are achieved by advances in medicine and technology with consequent subjection to more frequent and more invasive procedures and surgery.

Kwentus *et al* (1985) in their discussion of pain in the elderly began as follows:

> 'Discomfort, suffering and pain are not consequences of normal ageing, yet the fallacy persists that pain is not only normal, but irreversible in the elderly.'

In the Brattberg study, those over 65 years old did not report pain as frequently as the middle-aged (Brattberg *et al*, 1989). The findings of studies of sensitivity to pain stimuli suggest that any differences between young and old people are small.

NURSING PEOPLE IN PAIN

Central to the focus of this book is the fact that medical and surgical patients reportedly have a high incidence of pain, and that investigations, treatment and some aspects of essential nursing care potentially inflict or add to existing pain. Many people in the community attempt to lead their lives while contending with a variety of recurrent and chronic pains.

What do we need to know in order to help people in pain? The distinction between two types of knowledge—'know that' and 'know how'—is generally accepted. The first type is concerned with what we know 'in our heads', that is the facts, what books say, what researchers find. Knowledge of the anatomy and physiology of pain pathways, of pain-producing (nociceptive) stimuli and pain-producing chemicals are examples of the 'know that' type.

The second type of knowledge or 'know how' generally means skill. To a large extent 'know how' is what we know 'in our bodies', or at least express in our bodies by verbal or non-verbal communication and movement.

There is, however, other knowledge which is crucial to our under-standing and success in pain management. This third type of knowledge is what we know 'in our hearts', what we believe—about the pain and about one another. We have called it simply 'knowing'. In many respects, it is more profound and fundamental to the rela-tionship of nurse and patient than either 'know that' or 'know how' (Table 2).

Table 2. Types of knowledge

'Know that'	Know in the head
'Know how'	Know in the body
'Knowing'	Know in the heart

The knowledge of the nurse or other carer regarding pain is only one side of the picture. There is at least one other 'knower', that is the person in pain. The patient knows about pain in general and about his or her pain in particular, may know what to do about it (at least to some extent), and certainly knows in the sense of believing things about pain. Bringing together our understanding, the patient's understand-ing and that of any or all of the other participants such as relatives, doctors and physiotherapists to provide coherent and therapeutic management of pain is a central and at times very difficult nursing task.

We hope that the following chapters will be of some use to the players in these dramas. However, it is perfectly possible to read a book without gaining much 'know that', and 'know how' can be presented and discussed but is only learned when we speak, act and practise skills for ourselves. Knowing in our hearts can only be known to us—but the presentation of some of the beliefs of others may help to clarify our own.

REFERENCES

Abu-Saad H (1984) Assessing children's responses to pain. *Pain* **19**: 163–171.
Bonica J (1982) Introduction—Narcotic analgesics in the treatment of cancer and post-operative pain. Symposium, proceedings Stockholm, 12–14 Nov 1980. *Acta Anaesthesioligica Scandinavica* **26** (supplement 74): 5–10.
Bonica JJ (1984) Labour pain. In Wall PD & Melzack R (eds) *Textbook of Pain*. Edinburgh: Churchill Livingstone.
Brattberg G, Thorslund M & Wikman A (1989) The prevalence of pain in a

general population. The results of a postal survey in a county of Sweden. *Pain* **37**: 215–222.

Cassel EJ (1982) The nature of suffering and the goals of medicine. *New England Journal of Medicine* **306** (11): 639–645.

Cassel EJ (1991) *The Nature of Suffering and the Goals of Medicine.* Oxford: Oxford University Press.

Copp LA (1974) The spectrum of suffering. *American Journal of Nursing* **74** (3): 491–495.

Copp LA (1985) Pain, ethics and the negotiation of values. In Copp LA (ed.) *Perspectives on Pain, Recent Advances in Nursing*, pp 137–150. Edinburgh: Churchill Livingstone.

Craig KD, McMahon RJ, Morison JDS & Zaskon C (1984) Developmental changes in infant pain expression during immunization injections. *Social Science and Medicine* **19** (12): 1331–1337.

Degenaar JJ (1979) Some philosophical considerations on pain. *Pain* **7**: 281–304.

Diamond AW & Coniam SW (1991) *The Management of Chronic Pain.* Oxford: Oxford University Press.

Donovan M, Dillon P & McGuire L (1987) Incidence and characteristics of pain in a sample of medical—surgical inpatients. *Pain* **30**: 69–78.

Frank A (1954) *The Diary of a Young Girl.* London: Pan.

Fraser RA, Hotz SB, Hurtig JB, Hodges SN & Moher D (1989) The prevalence and impact of pain after day-care tubal ligation surgery. *Pain* **39**: 189–201.

Jensen TS & Rasmussen P (1989) Phantom pain and related phenomena after amputation. In Wall PD & Melzack R (eds) *Textbook of Pain*, 2nd edn, pp 508–521. Edinburgh: Churchill Livingstone.

Kwentus JA, Harkins SW, Lignon N & Silverman JJ (1985) Current concepts of geriatric pain and its treatment. *Geriatrics* **40** (4): 48–55.

Lewis CS (1940) *The Problem of Pain*, p 72. Glasgow: Collins.

Lipowski ZJ (1970) Physical illness, the individual and the coping processes. *Psychiatry in Medicine* **1** (2): 91–101.

McCaffery M (1972) Nursing Management of the Patient in Pain. Philadelphia: JB Lippincott.

McCaffery M & Beebe A (1989) Pain. *Clinical Manual for Nursing Practice*, pp 11–12. St Louis: CV Mosby.

Melzack R (1973) *The Puzzle of Pain*, p 13. Harmondsworth: Penguin.

Melzack R (1984) The Myth of Painless Childbirth. *Pain* **19**: 321–337.

Melzack R (1990) John J. Bonica Distinguished Lecture. The Gate Control Theory 25 years later: new perspectives on phantom limb pain. *Pain* (supplement 5): S254.

Melzack R, Kinch RA, Dobkin P, Lebrun M & Taenzer P (1984) Severity of labour pain: influence of physical as well as psychological variables. *Canadian Medical Association Journal* **130**: 579–584.

Merskey H (1967) *Pain: Psychological and Psychiatric Aspects.* London: Baillière Tindall & Cassell.

Merskey H (1980) Some features of the history of the idea of pain. *Pain* **9**: 3–8.

Rigge M (1990) Pain research on prevalence of pain in Britain. *Which? Way to Health* April, 66–68.

Royal College of Surgeons of England, College of Anaesthetists (1990) Commission on the provision of surgical services. Report of the Working Party on Pain After Surgery.

Schechter NA (1984) Recurrent pains in children: an overview and an approach. *Pediatric Clinics of North America* **31** (5): 949–968.

Seers CJ (1987) Pain, anxiety and recovery in patients undergoing surgery. PhD Thesis, University of London.

Seers CJ (1989) Patients' perception of acute pain. In Wilson-Barnett J & Robinson S (eds) *Directions in Nursing Research*, pp 107–116. London: Scutari Press.

Sofaer B (1983) Pain relief—the core of nursing practice. *Nursing Times*, **79** (47): 38–42.

Sternbach RA (1968) *Pain, a Psycophysiological Analysis*. New York: Academic Press.

Sternbach RA (1970) Strategies and tactics in the treatment of patients with pain. In Crue BL (ed.) *Pain and Suffering*, pp 176–185. Springfield, Ill: CC Thomas.

Tyrer SP (ed.) (1992) *Psychology, Psychiatry and Chronic Pain*. Oxford: Butterworth-Heinemann.

2

The Nurse and the Person in Pain

The relationship of patients and nurses can have an important and distinctive part to play in the care of people in pain. Firstly, because of early contact with patients, nurses are often the first health-care professionals to encounter the person in pain. Secondly, because their contact with patients is sustained, nurses may be the ones to identify the problem of uncontrolled pain. Thirdly, there are skills that the nurse ideally possesses that may be important to effective pain management: these include the ability to establish a trusting relationship, often quickly and in difficult circumstances, and the ability to help the person in pain communicate necessary information about their pain to others. These skills are crucial when exploring the isolation experienced by some people in pain.

The effects of pain, particularly unrelieved persistent pain, can be to imprison the sufferer. Not only may pain result in curtailment of freedom, but it may also create a barrier between the patient and others. The isolation experienced by some people in pain and the consequences of that isolation are explored in order to identify an often hidden but potentially pivotal role of the nurse in the care of people in pain.

PAIN ISOLATES

Pain separates in two directions—the person inside the prison of pain from those outside, and those outside pain from those inside. Pain is privately experienced. Pain, as an interior landscape, is a separate world not populated by others, even when the external world is shared. Pain is known by others only when information about it is communicated by the one experiencing it. Knowing by others is once removed. As nurses, we use cues or our intuition to alert us to the existence of pain. Cues about acute pain are frequently available to the outsider, but in chronic pain the body adapts, and often vegetative depressive signs are the only indicators available to the observer. Flattened affect and lethargy give no clues that pain is present, especially if the person observing does not know the usual personality and activity of the person in pain. Therefore, unless information about pain's existence is deliberately sought or shared, it may remain invisible. To the observer, it does not exist. Others' ignorance of pain can create for the person experiencing it an acute sense of loneliness.

Severe or chronic pain also isolates because it captures concentration and is insistent in its demand for attention and energy. Preoccupation with pain may render the one experiencing it unavailable to engage in social interaction or activities. Severe acute pain notoriously results in this isolating preoccupation. For example, a woman in the second stage of labour can only focus on what is happening to her, so may express irritation with any distractions surrounding her, including her partner. Not only does pain often force choices about activities, but may interfere with activities that promote or support social contact, such as eating and conversing.

In the other direction, pain can be the reason that friends, family and professional carers separate themselves from the person in pain. All may find it difficult to relate to such a person, especially if they have repeatedly failed in their attempts to alleviate or control the pain. The continuing distress of the person in pain is evidence of ineffectual knowledge and skills, and may lead to a sense of frustration that can be unintentionally communicated verbally and non-verbally (Herth, 1990; McLeod Clark, 1983). Not all pains are presently able to be relieved, and the person in pain may be avoided, physically and emotionally, to minimize reminders of powerlessness. Thus the isolation can be compounded by abandonment.

People in pain may also remain imprisoned when we believe that pain must always have an identifiable physical cause. If a physical cause cannot be found to explain the existence and severity of someone's experience, the pain (and the person in pain) may be dismissed by the 'experts' as not real and so not addressed seriously. Separation or splitting of the person and their pain may occur when the pain becomes the exclusive focus of the attention and activity of health professionals. A diagnosis describing the cause and symptoms may focus expertise on the pathology, to the exclusion of the person who is ill. The same thing happens to patients when the technological methods of monitoring their condition become the focus of attention, rather than the patient; the machine becomes more real than the person. Cassel (1982) describes the suffering that is created by splitting the physical, emotional and spiritual components of pain:

> Therefore, so long as the mind–body dichotomy is accepted, suffering is either subjective and thus not truly 'real'—not within medicine's domain—or identified exclusively with bodily pain. Not only is such an identification misleading and distorting, for it depersonalizes the sick patient, but it is itself a source of suffering. It is not possible to treat sickness as something that happens solely to the body without thereby risking damage to the person.

Self-doubt may be added to the vulnerability felt by the person who experiences pain but who is not acknowledged to have real pain by the 'experts', thus enhancing the patient's feelings of being alone, of being on the other side of certainty.

In summary, pain may separate the person by its private, subjective nature and by its insistent demand for attention. Pain can also lead to a sense of alienation when the physical aspects of pain are allowed exclusively to define its reality. If the pain continues to be uncontrolled, the one suffering it may be abandoned by everyone, including the nurses, thus adding to the sense of loneliness.

IMPLICATIONS OF ISOLATION IN PAIN

The fact that the person in pain may experience isolation raises several concerns. One concern focuses on the resources available for coping in pain. Being cut off from others, for whatever reason, results in a finite reservoir of personal strength and resources with which to confront and manage the pain. In the short term or in mild pain, the pain may be confronted without exhausting personal strength or needing external resources; but in situations of severe or enduring pain, the energy and resources that were originally present may become exhausted, leaving the person vulnerable to breakdown and dysfunction. It is this disintegration and dysfunction that often results in a poor quality of life for people with intractable pain. These individuals are so bound and consumed by their pain that they have nothing left with which to live in a satisfying manner—unable to sustain energy to relate to others or perform activities beyond those necessary to maintain life.

Another concern raised by this isolation is suggested in Herth's study of hope in terminally ill people. Herth (1990) found that whilst some strategies fostered hope, others threatened it. One threat to hope was emotional withdrawal by others who remained physically present; terminally ill people found this worse than physical withdrawal because the others' presence served as a reminder of the alienation and loss. Uncontrolled pain and discomfort coupled with isolation can lead to fatigue and a lack of energy to invest in the process of sustaining hope (Vaillot, 1970).

SKILLED COMPANIONSHIP

Given the isolation and abandonment that may be part of the experience of pain, an important and powerful activity of the nurse becomes that of 'being with' the person in pain. Even when we are unable to eliminate pain, loneliness can be overcome; and this may crucially affect the outcome of any of the pain control strategies that are offered. There are three tasks that make up this role:

1. Entering into the experience and establishing a presence.
2. Sustaining the connection.
3. Helping the person to make other connections.

Entering the experience

Earlier, the private nature of pain was raised to explain the isolation that pain may create. The nurse must find a way to know about the experience of the person in pain. Even if the other person's pain is a result of a commonly experienced condition, such as surgery, giving birth, arthritis or toothache, their experience is *unique*, depending upon such factors as personality, understanding of the cause and outcome of the pain, previous experiences with pain and cultural background. Thus the first step for the nurse in attempting to enter into the experience of the person in pain is to understand that this particular situation is unique. While knowledge and experience may sensitize us to what could be the experience of the person in pain, the particular situation must be explored to understand what *this* person is experiencing. The goal is to share the same perception of pain, and if that is not possible, to reduce the gap between the different perceptions of the patient and the nurse.

The nurse who 'knows' about pain and the accompanying aloneness is thus able to look through the prison bars. This looking through the bars to the person inside the pain experience is knowing in one's head and heart about pain and isolation. However, there is more that the nurse uses and offers to the person in pain.

The nurse brings to the encounter not only an acknowledgement that pain exists—looking through the bars to the person who is alone in their experience—but a concern to know and understand how pain is affecting this particular person. The facts—the duration, intensity, location and precipitating factors—can be interpreted in terms of a person's way of life: how the pain influences their living, their ability to function, relate to others and pursue interests. In essence, the nurse tries to understand the relationship between the pathology of pain and the lived experiences of the individual. Knowing about the meaning and consequences of pain allows the nurse to enter the prison and be alongside the person in pain. Before any therapeutic intervention has been attempted, the person in pain is no longer alone.

Benner and Wrubel (1989) used a nurse's description of an instance of this. The event took place in a busy clinic, a crowded space without much privacy. An older woman in a wheelchair came to the clinic with her daughter. She had severe rheumatoid arthritis with multiple deformities creating functional problems and pain. The nurse obtained some background information about the patient, then asked her if she used the wheelchair to get around. The response to that seemingly innocent question of fact provoked a 'flood of expression'. It transpired that this was the first time she had used a wheelchair. While the nurse had thought her extremely disabled from her arthritis, she had somehow managed to cope—getting around the house, caring for her family, carrying out a job—without 'having to resort to the symbolic state of being in a wheelchair'. The nurse commented at this point on a shift in the level of the interaction.

> Right away, that put us in touch with each other, and the encounter shifted to an emotional level. We were talking about feelings right from the beginning, before I had found out much about her.
> It's hard to express, but there is a sense when you feel that you are making contact with the patient . . . You understand *what they are* . . . [author's italics].

The nurse then continued a physical assessment, exploring the extent of pain and deformity from the patient's arthritis while making tentative statements about her functioning, such as 'I can tell that this must be really painful right now', 'It looks as if you haven't been able to use this hand for a long time', and 'This must be really difficult when you take a bath'. These comments invited the woman to elaborate on her experience, problems and ways of coping. The nurse was conveying the message 'I really am trying to understand how your life is affected'. The patient became more emotional, perhaps because she had never really discussed anything with anyone beyond 'This knee hurts' and 'This finger is swollen'. She had never talked about what the symptoms meant to her. She had never said: 'This means that I can't go to the bathroom by myself, put my clothes on, even get out of bed without calling for help.'

When the examination was finished the nurse said something like: 'Rheumatoid arthritis really has not been nice to you'. The lady burst into tears and said:

> 'You know, no one has ever talked about it as a personal thing before, no one's ever talked to me as if this were a thing that mattered, a personal event.'

In this encounter, the nurse not only gathered information about pain and the limited range of joint movements, but attempted to put herself in the patient's place by trying to 'know' about living life with arthritis. In presenting her perceptions as statements needing validation by the patient, the nurse voiced interest and concern about the impact of arthritis on her life and gave permission for the woman to talk about this area of her experience. Then by answering an open-ended question, about help with dressing in the morning, the woman was enabled to share for the first time what it meant to live with her disease.

This interaction demonstrated the way in which the nurse asked permission to know what living with pain was like. The patient's response to the question concerning the use of the wheelchair was a strong clue that she was trying to live as normally as possible within a difficult situation. The nurse's continuing exploration of how arthritis was experienced by the woman was a sign of caring that won the nurse permission from the patient to enter her isolated existence of pain.

Once the nurse has entered and established a presence, that presence needs to be maintained if the nurse's resources are to become available to the patient.

Sustaining the connection, maintaining the presence

Davies and Oberle (1990), in their intensive research with an expert nurse in palliative care, identified six dimensions of the supportive role. One of these is connecting, that is 'getting in touch' with the patient. Whilst it involves such activities as establishing credentials, explaining roles and obtaining information, it also means getting to know the person in a much deeper sense. An activity essential to connecting (getting close) is establishing trust, for as these workers noted, until trust is developed, connecting will not occur or (by implication) be sustained.

In an exploration of the concept of trust, Meize-Gochowski (1984) noted several factors that constitute trust. These include reliability (consistent behaviour) and confidence (freedom from uncertainty and doubt). Competence is also a component of developing trust. Allied to competence is the attempt to understand, which then leads the patient to believe that the nurse will help in time of need.

One outcome of trust includes an open and honest relationship between two people that can tolerate the exposure and exploration of uncomfortable or potentially threatening issues, such as increasing dependence brought about by the pain and deformity. The goal of exploring these areas is the hope of finding some way to understand and eliminate or minimize the difficulties that result from the pain. Even if little can be done to alter the problem, then the fact that there are two to share the load, lightens it. This is an answer to the concern raised earlier, about one of the consequences of isolation, of the patient only having a limited perspective or reservoir of resources. With two people, there is reason to suppose that the available resources will be expanded. The competent nurse brings the resources of knowledge and skills as well as a presence, a 'being with' the person in pain. Campbell (1984) called nursing 'skilled companionship', a companionship that at least reduces isolation and may even overcome it.

Helping make other connections

Once trust is established between the nurse and the patient, another resource of the nurse is knowledge about the skills possessed by other members of the multiprofessional team. The nurse is in a position to assist in connecting to (communicating with) other people who can be helpful.

Summary

How can a nurse come alongside the person in pain? First, before any words are spoken, much is communicated about the nurse's attitude to the person in pain. Direct eye contact, a sense of quiet and undistracted attention to the patient communicate the importance that the nurse places on this person and their concerns. The use of open questions and tentative statements allows the person in pain to share what is important and meaningful to them. It is this openness that sanctions or legitimizes for the patient, areas for shared exploration. Closed or leading questions, that is questions that predefine a range of responses, implicitly convey to the person in pain that responses from within a particular range are expected and cast doubt on whether it is permissible to raise other matters that may be important to them.

Checking back with the person in pain about what has been heard helps to narrow the perceptual gap betwen the nurse and patient about such important areas as the meaning of pain and the priorities in respect of its management. Validating or checking back communicates to the person in pain that their experiences and interpretations are being taken seriously. Many people find it difficult to translate what they experience into words. So checking back also becomes a way to assist the person in pain to give expression to their experience.

Skilful communication can thus convey the important messages 'I care about you' and 'I am trying to hear what you are saying'. These two messages are keys that can open the prison that pain can create.

REFERENCES

Benner P & Wrubel J (1989) *The Primacy of Caring: Stress and Coping in Health and Illness*, pp 10–11. Menlo Park: Addison-Wesley.

Campbell AV (1984) *Moderated Love: A Theology of Professional Care*. Society for the Propagation of Christian Knowledge, London.

Cassel EJ (1982) The nature of suffering and the goals of medicine. *New England Journal of Medicine* 306: 639–645.

Davies B & Oberle K (1990) Dimensions of the supportive role of the nurse in palliative care. *Oncology Nursing Forum* 7 (1): 87–94.

Herth K (1980) Fostering hope in terminally-ill people. *Journal of Advanced Nursing* 15: 1250–1259.

McLeod Clark J (1983) Nurse–patient communications—an analysis of recorded conversations from cancer wards. In Wilson-Barnett J (ed.) *Nursing Research: Ten Studies in Patient Care*. Chichester: John Wiley.

Meize-Gochowski R (1984) An analysis of the concept of trust. *Journal of Advanced Nursing* 9: 563–572.

Vaillot M (1970) Hope: the restoration of being. *American Journal of Nursing* 70 (2): 268–273.

3

The Nature and Meaning
of Pain

Knowledge about the nature and meaning of pain is crucial to our understanding of people in pain, and therefore to our ability to get alongside them. Some of the knowledge and beliefs that may form the basis of the skilled companionship of nursing are discussed in this chapter and listed in Table 1.

Table 1. Some aspects of pain.

The neurophysiology of pain
The experience of pain
The expression of pain
The meaning of pain
Self-knowledge

The complex phenomena of pain cannot always be captured by simplistic explanations, and scientific knowledge is provisional (Popper, 1972). For these reasons it could be potentially misleading to present current understanding as dogma. Advances in knowledge will hopefully result in improvement of assessment, prevention, care and treatment of pain in each succeeding generation.

CURRENT PAIN THEORIES

The neurophysiology of pain

Neurophysiological knowledge about pain is being developed and expanded at a rate that may make today's fact tomorrow's fallacy. The message emerging from the writings of those who study pain is that the more anatomical and physiological knowledge they acquire the less dogmatic they are willing to be about, for example, dedicated pain pathways, receptors and transmitters. Melzack (1990) stated that:

> In 25 short years (since Gate Control Theory was published in 1965) we have come a long way—from peripheral specificity to brain specialisation of enormous complexity.

Advances in science have had both a humbling and a liberating effect on our understanding of ourselves. Views of human function have sometimes been limited to analogy with the prevailing technology. Mechanistic views of 'man as machine' have never provided wholly satisfactory insights. Hard-wiring and 'telephone exchange' analogies of the nervous system have been modified. Even the more sophisticated comparisons with computer technology prove inadequate as explanations of human functioning.

We cannot ignore anatomy and physiology just because its frontiers are being expanded and refined, however. Successful nursing of patients in pain requires an understanding of the *implications* of anatomical and physiological knowledge. As discussed in Chapter 1 of this book, nurses have to understand many languages, including the language about the body used by physiologists, anatomists and medical practitioners, and those experiencing pain.

The experience of pain

There are many dimensions to the human pain experience, including the site and extent of pain, its intensity, the way it changes over time, and other symptoms (such as nausea) which may accompany it. Definitions and classifications of pain arise from this knowledge, for example of acute, chronic and intermittent pain. This knowledge can be gained from reading anecdotal and research descriptions of pain, listening to and observing patients and recalling our own experiences. Such knowledge leads us to abandon certainty, embrace uncertainty and live with unpredictability and the excitement of probability—as we do automatically in other areas of our lives such as social behaviour. In place of a typical or standard experience of pain, we have a range of possible experiences: for example, the experience of myocardial infarction may be of chest pain, chest tightness, arm pain, indigestion-like sensation or no pain at all. We are thus free to believe our patients, what they say and how they behave, and to utilize our own intuitions without making our assessment observations fit into a straitjacket of what the patient *should* say, feel or do in the circumstances—according to the textbooks.

It is crucial to separate absolute from probabilistic knowledge about the experience of pain. Individual patients have absolute knowledge about their pain. They have *their* pain—not necessarily the pain typically experienced in their disease. This is why McCaffery's definition of pain—'Pain is whatever the experiencing person says it is, and exists whenever he says it does'—is so important (McCaffery, 1972). We have, or can acquire, probabilistic knowledge about pain; for example, the percentage of people who experience pain in their left arm at the time of a myocardial infarction. This may help us and the patient to understand what is happening and what may alleviate the pain, why and how. Such knowledge will certainly enable us to make a more educated prediction of the possible pain of those with whom we cannot converse.

The meaning of pain

Profound questions about the meaning of pain rank with the great religious and philosophical questions about the meaning of life. Why are we here? What is our life about? Why do we experience pain? These questions cannot be answered by any amount of increase in knowledge of neurology. Such knowledge may provide clues as to how but not why pain is felt. The meaning of pain becomes a compelling issue to the person experiencing it. The answer he or she gives will fundamentally alter experience of and responses to pain. The word 'pain' is derived from the Greek *poine*, meaning punishment. A person who believes that pain is punishment for past wickedness may well decide to keep quiet about it or refuse pain relief. Understanding the religious or philosophical views of our patients may be a prerequisite to understanding their interpretations of pain.

However, there are less weighty and more pragmatic questions about the meaning of pain. What is pain indicating physically? The answer generally given to this question is that pain is an indication of injury, tissue pathology or disease, although as mentioned before this is not always so (e.g. psychogenic pain, and a number of chronic pains), and the onset of, for example, some visceral pain comes too late in the disease process to be a warning signal (Le Riche, 1939). Many chronic pains, including some back pain and headaches, cannot be traced to either injury or disease (Wall and Jones, 1991).

Another meaning of pain concerns the consequence pain has for the sufferer. Does increasing pain mean that death is close? Does recurrence of pain mean that discharge from hospital will be postponed? Does persistent pain mean that the sufferer will have to give up work, sports or caring for their family? These are some of the spoken and unspoken questions in the mind of many a patient. In summary, to nurse people in pain requires an understanding of philosophical, biological and psychosocial meanings of pain (Table 2).

Table 2. The meanings of pain.

Philosophical
Biological
Psychosocial

Self-knowledge

We cannot remove ourselves, our own attitudes, beliefs and experiences, from the situation. The myth that pain assessment is objective has to be abandoned. The lens through which we view our patients is tinted by our conceptions and misconceptions about pain. It may be difficult to change our beliefs, but it is perfectly possible to become more aware of our prejudices.

Perhaps when we report to one another on the condition of patients we could discuss how and why we came to our conclusions about the person with pain. We could try in a non-judgemental way to be open in sharing our thought processes with one another. For example, we could recall and discuss our family codes of behaviour regarding pain. What behaviour was encouraged and admired when we were hurt as children? Are the beliefs of our family, our school, our friends or our colleagues the only correct and possible ones?

The promotion of reflection as a learning strategy is discussed by Fish *et al* (1991). One of the authors (M.F.) learned as a student in the 1950s that hierarchies of pain corresponded to the extent of surgery. For example, 'major' surgery such as abdominoperineal resection of the rectum supposedly caused more severe pain than 'minor' surgery such as appendicectomy. The number of postoperative doses of opiates prescribed *a priori* was decided on this basis. What was assumed to follow from this dogma was that patients could be judged as minimizers (stoics or heroes) or exaggerators (hypochondriacs). Such beliefs are abandoned with difficulty; indeed, one can still find texts in which headache is given as an illustration of a mild pain and cancer pain as illustration of severe pain. The reverse may be true.

We like to believe that we are rational and hold to our views consistently, but this may not be entirely true. Sometimes we may be amazed at our own reactions when we speak, act, or feel in ways we would not have predicted. We may also be ambivalent. For example, when we are not in pain we think maybe it is ennobling; when we do have pain we neither feel ennobled nor wish to be ennobled that way; but afterwards we may feel that we did learn something about what it is to be part of humanity.

It is said that all nurses should be patients so that they can understand what it is like. However, the experience of accidental injury, surgery and any other pain-provoking situation can be misleading if we think everyone will experience pain as we did. Holm *et al* (1989) found some evidence that nurses' personal experiences did influence their ratings of patients' pain. One of the authors thought the pain of cystitis was 'a joke really' because it was first described as a trivial honeymoon condition—experience radically changed this view! Patient behaviour can also modify our views of pain. The excruciating pain of ureteric colic from oxalic acid stones was learned from a patient who begged us, the nurses, to pray for him. He was obviously terrified at the prospect of the next episode of pain. This in fact confirmed text book descriptions of ureteric colic.

Beliefs are modifiable by personal and nursing experience and by reading about and discussing the beliefs of other people. The most useful and important belief is arguably that the experience of pain is not reliably predictable from either the cause or the apparent lack of cause.

NEUROPHYSIOLOGICAL KNOWLEDGE ABOUT PAIN

Much anatomical and physiological knowledge about pain has been gained by experimentation upon animals and humans in laboratory settings. Increasingly, understanding has arisen from investigation and observation of patients in pain. The implications of such research findings for nursing depend upon the extent to which the anatomy and physiology of other species such as guinea-pigs or cats correspond to that of humans, the similarity and differences between laboratory-induced and 'real life' pain, and the specific pathology and typicality of the observed patients in pain.

Pain research has focused upon four theoretical positions. (A theory can be defined as a set of statements that specify the relationship between two or more concepts in order that a problem or the nature of something may be understood more fully. It may describe, explain or predict.) The four theories can be expressed as follows. Pain is experienced *as if*:

1. There is a direct, dedicated nerve 'hot line' from the site of injury to the brain—*specificity theory*.
2. A summation of nerve impulses occurs over time and/or space in non-specific nerves—*pattern theories*.
3. A modifiable open/closed mechanism exists in the nervous system (spinal cord)—*gate control theory*.
4. A continuously active nervous system modifies input and output, reception and response—*post gate control theories*.

These theories reflect a progression in knowledge. All have or have had partial explanatory value or apply to different pain phenomena. The last two theories are more comprehensive than the first two.

Specificity theory

The specificity theory was based on the assumption that pain was perceived following injury because there was a single, dedicated, hard-wired system of afferent nerves which carried messages from specific pain receptors in the periphery to a pain centre in the brain (Wall, 1989b). Descartes (1644) captured the idea beautifully in his analogy of bellringing: pull the rope at the bottom and the bell will ring in the belfry. Stub your toe or hammer your fingernail, and specificity theory apparently makes absolute sense.

The simple idea proposed is that specific nerve endings in the skin and other tissues respond exclusively to nociceptive (pain-producing) stimuli; that afferent nerves carry this information to specialized parts of the dorsal horn of the spinal cord, and thence via the anterolateral spinothalamic tract to the thalamus or pain centre in the brain, and to the relevant part of the sensory cortex. This appealing theory is now considered wholly oversimplified. The concept of a single, isolated neural system constituting *the pain mechanism* is dismissed by Wall

(1989a) as a 'moribund sterile corpse'. There are many phenomena that this theory fails to illuminate. For example, variability in pain threshold, the absence of pain when injury occurs during overwhelmingly interesting and exciting activities, the return of pain following nerve severance, cordotomy and even thalamotomy, and phantom limb pain.

Pattern theories

Pattern theories relate the perception of pain to patterns of impulses in the nervous system rather than to impulses in dedicated pain pathways. The patterns may be temporal (in time) or spatial (in space). Hebb (1949) suggested that pain is a disrupted pattern of firing in the thalamus. Weddell (1955) proposed that pain occurred when particular spatial or temporal patterns of impulses were generated in afferent nerves by intense stimulation of non-specific receptors. Failure to identify specific nociceptive afferents in the viscera made this a particularly attractive theory to explain visceral pain (Malliani *et al*, 1984). In an attempt to understand and explain the existence and persistence of pain following damage to or severance of the spinal cord, Melzack and Loeser (1978) proposed that neuron pools at many levels of the spinal cord or brain can act as 'pattern-generating mechanisms', as when deafferentation has occurred in paraplegia. Pattern theories may explain some chronic or recurrent pains which occur when there are nerve lesions. The triggering of or spontaneous activity in reverberating neuronal circuits are speculative explanations. The many potential influences on pattern-generating mechanisms as discussed by Melzack (1981) invoke the gate control theory.

Gate control theory

The observation of Head and Sherrin (1905) that the epicritic system (sensibility to gentle stimulation) inhibited the protopathic system (sensibility to pain) of nerves foreshadowed the idea of a gate.

Gate control theory was first published by Melzack and Wall (1965). The theory proposed that a neural mechanism in the dorsal horns of the spinal cord acts like a gate, effectively increasing or decreasing the flow of nerve impulses from peripheral nerves to the central nervous system (Figure 1). They stated that:

> The degree to which the gate increases or decreases sensory transmission is determined by the relative activity in large diameter (A-beta) and small diameter (A-delta and C) fibres and by descending influences from the brain.

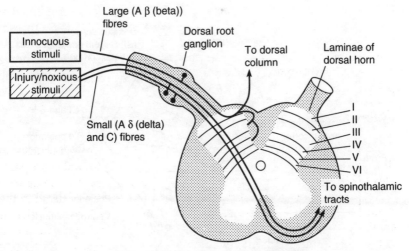

Figure 1. *Schematic diagram of the spinal cord.*

Wall (1984) wrote of gate control theory as follows:

> It incorporates the now accepted fact that the messages concerned with pain transmitted from the first central cells in the spinal cord depend upon three factors:
>
> 1. The arrival of nociceptive messages.
> 2. The convergent effect of other peripheral afferents which may exaggerate or diminish the effects of the nociceptive message.
> 3. The presence of control-systems within the CNS (Central Nervous System) which influence the first central cells. We emphasise that convergent controls decide the fate of arriving messages as they pass through every level of the central nervous system and eventually produce reaction, sensation and movement.

Gate control theory helps to integrate the known modifications of pain perception by higher centres such as emotional (happiness, fear) and cognitive (knowledge, meaning) influences. Descending inhibitory systems arising from, for example, raphe nuclei, the reticular formation and the hypothalamus are a rich source of hypotheses (Figure 2).

Post gate control theories

Post gate control theories modify and elaborate ideas inherent in gate control theory, on the one hand adding sophistication and on the other

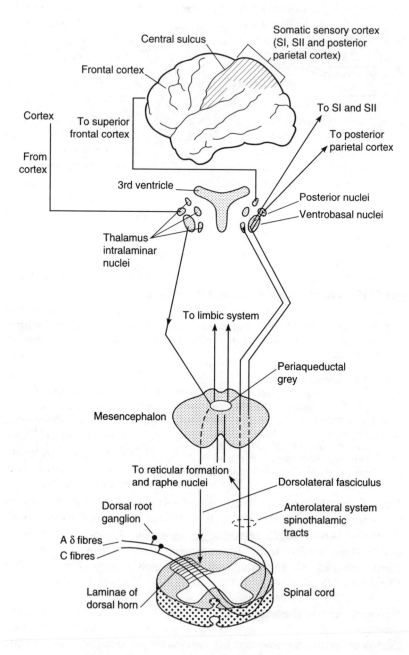

Figure 2. *Central nervous system, pathways and structures.*

lessening dogma about the explanation of pain phenomena in humans. Gone are the days when findings were facts, theories were truths and one effect was produced by one cause! Such simplicity was of limited value to people in pain when the interpretation of research findings did not fit the reality and complexity of human experience.

There has been a particular interest in the role of naturally occurring chemicals released at the site of injury from damaged cells, such as prostaglandins and bradykinin, and from nerve endings, such as substance P and 5-hydroxytryptamine (Messing and Lytle, 1977). One of the most exciting research trails has been that of the endorphins, endogenous opioid peptides (Fields and Basbaum, 1984) and their relationship to descending modulation of pain.

The importance of all such research has been the achievement of greater understanding of the mechanisms of pain and the therapeutic actions of drugs such as aspirin, morphine and naloxone and the potential to develop new interventions. Hypotheses such as the depletion of central nervous system 5-hydroxytryptamine have been suggested as a basis for sleep disturbance, lowered pain threshold and depression in chronic pain (Sternbach, 1984).

Many hypotheses about the possible way in which non-invasive and psychosocial interventions may work arise from this research. However, as with the four theories of which they are an integral part, simplicity has given way to complexity. Tissue chemicals and neurotransmitters are considered to be less exclusive in their actions than specificity theory would require, and there is a hot debate about endorphins (Woolf and Wall, 1983).

What are the views and disputes three decades after gate control theory began a revolution? The whole edifice has not toppled. There are nerve endings that respond to potentially harmful stimuli; there are chemicals that when released from damaged tissue and from nerves alter sensitivity locally and far away from the site of injury; there are afferent nerves with cell bodies in the dorsal root ganglia and fibres synapsing in the dorsal horn of the spinal cord that are activated from the nociceptors; and the anterolateral spinothalamic tract does transmit information from the dorsal horn to the thalamus. What is no longer accepted is that these pathways and chemicals are dedicated solely to pain phenomena. Also other structures and chemicals are involved in pain perception.

Nerve endings are now known to be less exclusive in their responses. Not only do some dorsal horn neurons have amoeboid-like changes in the area of skin to which they respond, but also if peripheral nerves are cut, the dorsal horn neurons that have lost their sensory input begin to respond to the nearest intact afferent—see Wall's discussion of the status of the dorsal horn (Wall, 1989b). Cut nerves attempt to regenerate with fine sprouts. 'These . . . generate impulses without any provocation, and are very easily stimulated by slight pressure. . . . They also become sensitive to chemicals, especially those emitted by the sympathetic nervous system' (Wall and Jones, 1991).

The actions of tissue chemicals and neurotransmitters are debated; transmission via the dorsal horn is complicated by multiple interconnections at all levels of the spinal cord. Information is passed via many neural tracts including the spinothalamic, spinoreticular, spinomesencephalic, spinocervical and dorsal tracts, such that activity is altered not only in thalamic nuclei and somatosensory cortex but also in other parts of the brain including the reticular system and the whole limbic system.

Science is beginning to endorse ideas that lay people have always believed. Pain is recognized as a subjective experience which cannot be adequately defined either by the stimulus or the response of humans.

A major benefit of the greater understanding of pain is that the pragmatic, humanistic, physically non-invasive and psychosocial actions of patients in pain, nurses, doctors, psychologists and physiotherapists have regained a respectability and validity formerly submerged by the successful but partial view of scientific reductionism. It should be noted that there is now a blurring of the mind–body dichotomy, and an overlap in the use of language by body and mind specialists.

The puzzles of pain

There are possible explanations for some of the puzzles of pain summarized in Table 3. The basic question which neurologists, psychologists, neurophysiologists, basic medical scientists, medical and nursing practitioners and patients are grappling with is this: why is the intensity, severity and total experience of human pain not predictable from the amount, type and location of tissue damage? The general answer is that the potential pain information enters an already active peripheral and central nervous system, the effects of which can be to block or admit, reduce or enhance, and interpret the significance of the incoming information. It is not a neuron that experiences pain, but a whole human being with memories, expectations, desires and intentions.

Table 3. Some puzzles of pain.

1. Some rare individuals fail to feel pain at all
2. Some pathological conditions result in either the loss of the ability to feel pain or enhanced pain, or both, e.g. diabetes
3. Pain can be experienced without any apparent cause
4. Pain can be felt in absent parts of the body, i.e. following amputation
5. Pain can be excruciating when tissue damage is minimal, e.g. ureteric stones
6. Pain can be absent following massive injuries
7. Pain can be felt (in localized places only) at the site of tissue damage
8. Pain can be felt far away from the site of the tissue damage
9. Pain can be felt all over the body
10. Pain can move around the body

Failure to feel pain

Some rare individuals fail to feel pain at all. This is termed *congenital insensitivity to pain*. Children with this disorder have severe difficulty in learning how to avoid physical damage such as bruises or cuts, and tend to die young with multiple damage to their body (Sternbach, 1963; Melzack, 1973). Bischoff (1979) reported that such people lack C fibres in their peripheral nervous system. Scadding (1989) described absence of small dorsal root ganglion cells and other peripheral neuropathies in such people.

Abnormality of pain sensation

Some pathologies result in the loss of the ability to feel pain or in enhanced pain, or in both states together, e.g. the diabetic 'painless–painful foot'.

There are a number of conditions that predispose to peripheral neuropathies, including drug effects (isoniazid), vitamin deficiencies (vitamin B), renal and thyroid failure, myeloma and alcoholism, as well as diabetes (Scadding, 1989). Peripheral sensory nerves are damaged in a variety of ways, resulting in changes of sensation. Pain and other sensations can be lost, but at the same time spontaneous sensations and pains may occur. Parts of the body, particularly the feet and hands, may feel odd, and unpredictably hot, cold, painful, painless, senseless, burning or dead. These abnormalities are thought to be dependent upon the exact nature of the nerve damage. When sensation is lost there is particular danger of injury being unnoticed. The terms *dysaesthesia* and *paraesthesia* are used to describe the strange mixtures of odd, excessive and absent sensations.

Pain without apparent cause

Pain can be experienced without any apparent cause. Sometimes there is a cause, but it is not discovered at the time. Sometimes the cause is neurogenic. Chronic pains that persist after healing has apparently occurred, such as postherpetic pain, may arise from permanent nerve damage (Dubuisson, 1989). Spontaneous activity in the nervous system may sometimes be an explanation. Sometimes the cause is psychological. Empathic pain may be an example of psychogenic pain. Empathy is the recognition of and entering into the feelings of another person. Anecdotal evidence leaves no doubt that some fathers-to-be feel 'labour pains', and many nurses, doctors and others including relatives or friends experience the pain of patients in the same parts of the body, although usually only fleetingly.

Many recurrent headaches and chronic backaches at present seem to fall into this category of 'pain without any discernible damage' (Wall and Jones, 1991). Part of the definition of pain given by Merskey (1979) states:

> Many people report pain in the absence of tissue damage or any likely pathophysiological cause. Usually this happens for psychological reasons. There is no way to distinguish their experience from that due to tissue damage, if we take (accept) the subjective report.

Phantom pain

Pain can be felt in absent parts of the body, i.e. following amputation. Sensations occurring following amputation are classified as phantom limb, phantom pain and stump pain (Merskey, 1986). Phantom sensations can occur following removal of a limb, nose, eyeball, tongue, teeth, penis, scrotum or breast (Jensen and Rasmussen, 1989), and following the gradual loss of a limb as in leprosy (Price, 1976). There are multiple explanations of the persistence or existence of phantom pain, including continued firing in severed peripheral nerves, consequent maintenance of input to the central nervous system, neuromas in the stump, and persistent spinal cord and brain activity.

Pain from minimal tissue damage

Pain can be excruciating when tissue damage is minimal e.g. ureteric stones. Different parts of the body have different nerve supplies, so that some parts such as the fingers and the tongue are more sensitive than other parts such as the back and abdominal skin. Directly stimulating a nerve, for instance by hitting the elbow (ulnar nerve) or by a photographic flashlight striking the retina can result in very severe pain without any apparent tissue injury.

Stretching of internal hollow organs such as the intestines, the ureters and the bile ducts can result in the most intolerable of pains even though the lining and wall of these structures is scarcely if at all damaged. The colicky pain is due to increased peristaltic action. Afferent fibres of the autonomic nervous system are involved in the transmission of sensation from these internal organs, but this does not explain why the pain experienced is so severe. Distension of the capsules of the liver and kidneys also gives rise to severe pain; and although the underlying pathology may indeed be serious, the actual damage to the capsule is not.

Injury without pain
Pain can be absent following massive injuries. Injury without pain is a paradoxical state, but one that occurs not only 'in the heat of battle' when conscious attention is focused on staying alive or winning the match, but is also experienced by between 28% and 53% of injured casualty patients (Melzack *et al*, 1982). The body is capable of producing a state of instantaneous analgesia at specific injured sites, allowing the injured person to carry on their current activity or to seek help and evaluate the consequences of injury in a detached manner.

There are reportedly three features that need explanation. One, that the pain-free state exists immediately; and two, that this analgesia is limited to the site of the injury, i.e. the rest of the body can still feel pain; and three, that eventually all patients do feel pain (Wall, 1989a). It is not clear what is happening in the nervous system—internal opiates may be produced, descending efferent nervous system responses may be triggered by such injuries—but explanations of this important and beneficial response to injury are presently debatable.

Localized pain
Pain can be felt at the site of the tissue damage in localized places only. This is what is most expected and most commonly experienced. Pain from skin and superficial injuries is precisely localized at the site of damage. An open gate and information transmission through peripheral and central nerves to the sensory cortex seem to explain this phenomenon.

Referred pain
Pain can be felt far away from the site of tissue damage. Pain that is felt in structures far away from the site of origin is called *referred* pain or *transferred* pain (Procacci and Zoppi, 1984). It classically arises when intense pain in viscera is prolonged, or following some musculoskeletal

injuries. Superficial referred pain to the skin is felt in the areas of the cutaneous distribution of spinal nerves (dermatomes) and deep referred pain is experienced in the areas of the muscle distribution of spinal nerves (myotomes) or bone (sclerotomes). Damage to nerve roots may give rise to pain in muscle, fascia and connective tissue if they have developed from the same embryonic mesoderm.

Pain all over the body
There are times when the whole body is hypersensitive, typically when a generalized viral infection such as influenza results in aching of all skeletal muscles. Severe, prolonged, intractable pains such as have been experienced by some terminal cancer patients (Le Shan, 1964) may result in pain being an all-consuming sensation.

Changing location of pain
Pain can move around the body. The way in which pain develops and changes in location and character is used to aid the diagnosis of intra-abdominal and thoracic pain. Typically, appendicitis pain is described as starting in the umbilicus and then being felt in the right iliac fossa. The particular segments of spinal thoracic and lumbar nerves involved are well understood, but the exact pattern of pain varies as does the anatomical position of the appendix (Blendis, 1989).

EXPERIENTIAL KNOWLEDGE OF PAIN

Experiential knowledge is concerned with the subjective phenomeno-logical experience of pain. This knowledge highlights both the unique-ness and the commonalities of pain experiences. Three aspects of pain are distinguishable by the human sufferer. These are sensory/perceptual, emotional/motivational and cognitive/evaluative (Melzack and Casey, 1968).

The *sensory/perceptual* aspect of pain concerns the discrimination of pain in time, space and intensity.

The *emotional/motivational* aspect of pain refers to the generally aversive negative feelings which motivate the behavioural responses to pain.

The *cognitive/evaluative* aspect of pain is concerned with the quality of knowing, evaluating, interpreting and conceptualizing pain (Table 4).

Table 4. The experience of pain.

Sensory/perceptual
  Site(s)
  Extent
  Intensity
  Timing
  Nature or quality
Emotional/motivational
  Feelings:
    Anxiety
    Anger
    Fear
    Sorrow
    Depression
    Fatigue
    Exhaustion
    Irritability
    Aggressiveness
  Actions:
    Avoidance
    Seek help
    Seek rest
    Seek seclusion
Cognitive/evaluative
  Evocation of past experiences and
  prediction of likely consequences
    Recognition
    Evaluation
    Interpretation

These three aspects of experience can occur concurrently or sequentially. Perceptual experience often predominates in acute pain. Emotional aspects may increasingly predominate with chronic pain. Evaluation occurs both instantaneously and in the long term.

Differences in these aspects are reflected in the definitions and classifications of pain. The International Association for the Study of Pain Sub-Committee on Taxonomy (1979) defined pain as 'an unpleasant sensory and emotional experience associated with actual or potential tissue damage or described in terms of such damage'. This stresses the bodily feeling and aversive nature of pain.

In 1987, the National Institutes of Health definition (Royal College of Surgeons of England, College of Anaesthetists, 1990) embraced the whole gamut of pain as follows:

Pain is a subjective experience that can be perceived directly only by the sufferer. It is a multidimensional phenomenon that can be described by pain location, intensity, temporal aspects, quality, impact and meaning. Pain does not occur in isolation but in a specific human being in psycho-social, economic and cultural contexts that influence the meaning, experience and verbal and non-verbal expression of pain.

Important differences in pain experience lead to broad classifications of types of pain (Table 5).

Table 5. Classification of pain.

Acute/chronic
Tractable/intractable
Useful/useless/harmful
Persistent/intermittent
Referred or transferred
Somatic/visceral
Phantom

Acute and chronic pain

The distinction between acute and chronic pain is very important. Not only do the physical responses differ but also the biological and social import. By far the majority of research has been on acute pain, but the greatest challenges to pain relief are cases of chronic pain. Cervero (1987) highlighted the issue thus:

Although visceral pain is the most common form of pain produced by disease and [accounts for] a substantial proportion of recurrent and persistent pain syndromes, yet little of the underlying neurophysiological mechanisms are understood as traditional pain studies examine immediate reactions of the central nervous system to acute skin injury.

Acute pain is described by Bonica (1982) as:

A constellation of unpleasant, perceptual and emotional experiences and associated autonomic (sympathetic) reflex responses and psychologic and behavioural reactions provoked by tissue damage inherent in injury or disease.

Melzack (1981) stated that acute pain is associated with a well-defined cause, has a characteristic time course and vanishes after healing. Carpenito (1983), in the American classification of nursing diagnoses, associated acute pain with a limited time (1 second to 6 months!) and its disappearance with healing or when the pain-provoking stimulus is removed.

Chronic pain, in contrast, is said to continue long after an injury has healed and may spread to adjacent and distant parts of the body (Melzack, 1981). The list of diagnoses associated with chronic pain given by Bonica (1982) suggest, however, that continuing tissue damage and incomplete healing may account for at least some chronic pains, including those of cancer, arthritis and peripheral and central neuropathies. Other chronic pains do not appear to be related to any discoverable injury or pathology (Wall and Jones, 1991).

Le Shan (1964), in an article about severe prolonged pain, graphically described the experience of unrelieved terminal cancer pain as resulting in the turning inwards of consciousness, the loss of time perspective, feelings of helplessness and of pain as threatening, alien and mean-ingless. Many other chronic pains may result in feelings of fatigue and exhaustion and in a preoccupation of the sufferer with pain and health.

Tractable and intractable pain

Instead of tying pain classification to the time course, it is sometimes more useful to distinguish between treatable pain and pain for which no therapy is effective (Wall, 1986), whether or not there is a clear organic diagnosis of its cause. Glyn (1987) defined intractable pain as pain of at least 1 month's duration that has not been relieved by conventional techniques. The pathologies of intractable pains cited by Wall are similar to those of chronic pains, and include deep tissue damage as in arthritis, low back pain and cystitis; peripheral nerve damage as in causalgia and amputation pains, and dorsal root damage as in arachnoiditis and brachial plexus avulsion (Wall, 1986).

Useful, useless and harmful pain

The distinction between useful, useless and harmful pain is crucial to decisions about the type and urgency of interventions, and is discussed in the section on the meaning of pain.

Persistent and intermittent pain

Pains may vary in intensity as noted by Domzal el al (1983), who stated that many painful diseases have definite patterns of circadian variation in the intensity of pain. The highest sensitivity to experimentally induced pain has been found to occur in the evening (Procacci *et al*, 1974). Likewise, intractable pain typically increases throughout the day, reaching a peak in the evening (Glyn *et al*, 1976). Musculoskeletal pains such as arthritis tend to be persistent even if varying in intensity. Other pains are intermittent, they come and go like the tides—indeed, sometimes with the tides! Some such pains arise from intermittent sudden exertion—the aftermath of sports activities or gardening, for instance. Other intermittent pains result from regular physiological rhythms such as monthly menstruation or the uterine contractions of labour. The timing of migraine and other headaches may or may not be regular or predictable (Diamond and Coniam, 1991). The periodicity of pain and the identification of possible precipitating factors are important aspects of pain assessment (Rasmussen, 1993).

Referred or transferred pain

When pain is felt in one part of the body but the cause is in another part, confusion can arise (see care study 2 on pp 150–152). If, for example, someone has a pain in the shoulder, this could be caused by an injured shoulder or could be referred from subdiaphragmatic pressure, e.g. a subphrenic abscess or cholecystitis. Fortunately, many transferred pains are correctly recognized by medical and nursing staff and can be understood by the sufferer. Commonly encountered pains include sciatic nerve compression giving rise to pain (and other sensations) in the buttock, leg and foot.

The pain of myocardial infarction (MI) is described as typically radiating from the centre of the chest or upper abdomen to feelings of constriction and heaviness around the chest and into the left arm. However, MI pain can differ from this typicality and may even be absent—the silent MI (Procacci and Zoppi, 1989).

Somatic and visceral pain

Both the anatomy and the experience of somatic and visceral pain differ (*somatic* refers to skin and musculoskeletal structures, and *visceral* to the internal organs of the thorax and abdomen). Cousins (1989) distinguished the major characteristics of somatic and visceral pain, stressing typical differences. The sufferer of visceral pain often has a problem in providing a clear description of the experience, as the site of visceral pain is difficult to pinpoint and the words used to describe the pain may be vague, e.g. 'pressure' or 'cramping' rather than 'sharp'. Visceral pain is more likely to be felt away from the site of disease, and may be less constant, or wax and wane in a periodic or intermittent fashion.

Symptoms of nausea and general malaise more frequently accompany visceral than somatic pain.

Phantom pain

It has become increasingly accepted that pain felt in an absent part of the body is just as real and perhaps more frustrating and frightening to the sufferer than many other pains. The most commonly experienced phantom pain follows limb amputation. The exact nature of pain differs from person to person but many people feel it in the distal (end) part of an amputated limb, experiencing a feeling of the hand or foot being squeezed or clenched with the nails digging into the flesh. Others may feel the absent part is in a distorted position which is painful (Brown, 1968). To have a painful limb removed surgically only to find pain still present seems a betrayal of reason.

Sensations of phantom limb in which the real or a distorted image is felt often accompany phantom pain. Phantom pain may persist or recur for years in a small percentage of amputees (Jensen and Rasmussen, 1989).

Labelling different types of pain in this way is useful in that it reminds us that experiences of pain vary widely. It may help in assessment to bear the classification in mind as the personal experience, likely cause and appropriate care and interventions will differ according to the type of pain.

THE EXPRESSION OF PAIN

Pain, like any other human experience, is capable of expression in three major ways, that is by physiological response, by behavioural response and by verbal description (Reading, 1984). A problem in interpreting pain research on animals is that only two ways of expression—physiological and behavioural—occur, along with non-verbal vocalizations. Nurses and others are faced by similar problems of interpretation when caring for babies, asphasic and unconscious people, and those whose language they do not share.

Physiological expressions

When a person is in pain a whole gamut of physiological activity is occurring in the nervous and other systems which is not open to scrutiny except by invasive procedures. However, the outcome of some of the changes in the autonomic nervous system can be observed or measured, and is felt by the sufferer. In acute pain it seems that this expression reflects predominant activity in the sympathetic nervous system and vagal inhibition. The result is that heart rate and stroke volume increase; the peripheral blood vessels constrict and blood pressure rises; palmar and plantar sweating occurs; glycogen is released from the liver into the blood circulation, and the motility of the gastrointestinal system is slowed. There are exceptions to this picture in that some visceral pains result in a fall in heart rate and blood pressure. Overall the immediate response to pain prepares a person for action. A most important fact, however, is that people in chronic pain usually do not have dramatic changes in physiology. Perhaps the body is incapable of maintaining these responses. A summary of these responses is given in Table 6.

Table 6. Physiological expressions of acute pain.

Heart rate Stroke volume Blood pressure	increase (or decrease in some visceral pains)

Peripheral vasoconstriction
Glycogen release from liver to blood
Inhibition of gastrointestinal motility
Pupil dilation
Palmar and plantar sweating
Alveolar ventilation and oxygen consumption increase

Behavioural expressions

By 'behavioural expression' is meant any non-verbal response to pain. The outcome of these behaviours are very important to the pain sufferer. Some behaviours may minimize the severity of pain, e.g. keeping still; some remove the cause of pain, e.g. running away; some reduce the pain, e.g. rubbing skin; and some clearly convey the experience of pain to other people, e.g. facial expressions (Le Resche, 1982).

Some behavioural responses are difficult, if not impossible, for the person in pain to control, for example the abdominal muscle wall guarding which occurs with peritonitis, and reflex withdrawal from extreme heat or fire. Other expressions such as rocking, rubbing or moaning are semiautomatic responses but can be controlled or stopped, at least for a time. The extent to which controllable non-verbal behavioural expressions of pain are displayed is to a large extent culturally determined. If these behavioural responses fail to extinguish pain then lay or professional help is likely to be sought. Some of the more common behavioural expressions are listed in Table 7, including those of children with chronic pain.

Table 7. Behavioural expressions of pain.

Bodily posture	Holding or protecting the part of body that hurts
Mobility	Local muscle spasm; stillness; hypermobility—rocking, rubbing, running, jumping
	Chronic pain: whole body tension; cautious movement
Vocalizations	Grunting, moaning, screaming
Facial expressions	Frowning, screwing up closed eyes; stretched open mouth
	Chronic pain: facial muscle tension
Accompanying symptoms	Nausea; sleep disturbance
	Chronic pain: appetite disturbance, e.g. dysphagia or hyperphagia; disruption of sleep pattern
Children with chronic pain	
Infants	Withdraw and develop eating and sleeping difficulties
Preschool children	Lose motor and toilet training milestones
School-age children	Become increasingly aggressive, or withdrawn or out of control
Adolescents	Become depressed, withdraw socially or develop oppositional behaviour

From Stoddard (1982).

Verbal expressions

Verbal expression of pain may be spontaneous or solicited and may refer to any aspect of the pain experience: sensory, emotional or cognitive. Although we stress throughout this book that the verbal expression of human pain is central to our understanding of people in pain, it has to be admitted that many people have difficulty in explaining their experiences clearly to others. In fact, a great deal of psychosocial research has been devoted to the development of ways of enhancing verbal expression (assessment tools). Verbal responses are culturally determined. This issue of culture and pain expression is discussed later in the book.

When nursing people in pain we may rely to some extent on their description to diagnose the likely cause. For example, if someone declines to use the word 'pain' but instead talks of 'pressure' or 'tightness' we may well presume the pain is visceral rather than somatic. The McGill–Melzack pain questionnaire (Melzack, 1975) contains words that refer to the extent and intensity of pain, other subjective feelings of pain, and the way it changes over time. Examples of these words are given in Table 8. Dubuisson and Melzack (1976) found that eight pain syndromes were distinguishable in a statistically significant way from the pain descriptions used. These were metastatic carcinoma, postherpetic neuralgia, phantom limb pain, toothache, degenerative disc disease, rheumatoid arthritis or osteoarthritis, labour pain and menstrual pain.

Table 8. Verbal expressions of pain.

Tone of voice different from normal
Length of utterances short or rambling
Concurrent vocalization such as 'Ough'
Choice of words including graphic analogies, e.g. 'like a knife cutting'

Examples of words from McGill pain questionnaire
  Extent, intensity:
    spreading, radiating, intense, mild, excruciating, sharp, agonizing, dull
  Other subjective feelings:
    drawing, squeezing, tearing, itchy, throbbing, gnawing, freezing, sickening, unbearable
  Changes over time:
    continuous, steady, constant, rhythmic, periodic, intermittent, brief, momentary, transient

In general the more overwhelming the experience of pain the less willing the sufferer is likely to be to give a lengthy verbal description. Aspects of the verbal expression of pain are listed in Table 8.

THE MEANINGS OF PAIN

As mentioned in the introduction to this chapter it is possible to distinguish three ways in which pain may have meaning to the sufferer: the philosophical and religious meaning, the biological meaning and the social meaning.

Philosophical and religious meanings

The philosopher Degenaar (1979) stated:

> In a sense one can say that the philosophical function of pain is its challenge to a person to become personally involved in what is happening and to respond in a creative way through meaning–giving activity.

People in pain, especially those whose pain arises unpredictably, are provoked to attempt to find answers to the questions, why? Why me? Why now?

Canon Autton, a hospital chaplain who has taken a particular interest in the problem of pain, wrote in 1986:

> Pain forces man to reflect, and it will be his inner attitude which will often shape his ability to cope with his pain experience and cultivate a powerful formative and transformative effect. . . . Pain can never be neutral; it impels a human being to make a personal decision, an act of will. He must take some attitude towards it, for pain demands a personal answer from the individual. As the common companion of birth, growth, disease and death, it is 'a phenomenon deeply intertwined with the very question of human experiences, and it often precipitates questioning the meaning of life itself' (Baken, 1968).

The search for and the attribution of meaning to pain is thus not only a necessary response but also a way of coping with pain. As Dr Cassel wrote in his article on the nature of suffering and the goals of medicine (Cassel, 1982):

> Meaning and transcendence offer two . . . ways by which the suffering associated with destruction of a part of personhood is ameliorated.

Cassel included unrelieved undiagnosed and overwhelming pains as potential threats to the integrity of the person.

Philosophical and religious meanings of life and pain are developed in the context of culture. Illich (1976) discussed the relationship of culture to pain. He suggested that:

To enable individuals to transform bodily pain into a personal experience, any culture provides at least four interrelated sub-programmes: words, drugs, myths and models.

Regarding the myths and models, Illich (1976) stated:

> Religious and mythic rationales for pain have appeared in all cultures: for the Muslims, it is *kismet*, God-willed destiny; for the Hindus, *karma*, a burden from past incarnations; for the Christians, a sanctifying backlash of sin. . . . In addition to myths, cultures always have provided examples on which behaviour in pain could be modelled: the Buddha, the saint, the warrior, or the victim.

Illich further suggested that the Western view of pain arose in European cultures which up to the seventeen century were rooted in classical Greek, Semitic and Christian ideologies. Although these ideologies differed in dogma they 'all saw pain as the bitter taste of cosmic evil, the manifestation of nature's weakness, of a diabolical will, or of a well-deserved divine curse'. Pain was to be suffered, alleviated and interpreted by the person affected; 'the idea of professional technical pain-killing was alien to all European civilisations'. The reasons for this point of view were:

1. Pain was man's experience of a marred universe, not a mechanical dysfunction in one of its subsystems (man).
2. Pain was a sign of corruption in nature, and man himself was a part of that whole.
3. Pain was an experience of the soul and this soul was present all over the body (Illich, 1976).

Twentieth-century pain sufferers also endow their experience of pain with their personal and culturally developed views. Metaphysical meanings of pain were illustrated by the research findings of Copp (1974). The thoughts of 148 inpatients in the USA, many in intensive care units, were sought while they were experiencing pain. More than half the sample viewed their pain as having some value as a personal challenge, something to fight and overcome, a spur to creativity, self-searching and increased understanding of others, and approximately one-quarter viewed pain as weakness in themselves or as punishment.

These philosophical and religious views of pain arose prior to the expansion of science and development of modern surgery. Metaphysical views of pain now coexist with mechanistic ones. Arguably mechanistic views have come to dominate. Illich (1976) explained this revolution in the following way:

> The campaign against pain as a personal matter to be understood and suffered got underway only when body and soul were divorced by Descartes. He constructed an image of the body in terms of geometry, mechanics or watchmaking, a machine that could be repaired by an engineer. For Descartes pain became a signal with which the body reacts in self-defence to protect its mechanical integrity. . . . Pain was reduced to a useful learning device: it now taught the soul how to avoid further damage to the body.

This leads to the biological meaning of pain.

Biological meaning

What is the biological point or purpose of experiencing pain? The most commonly held view of pain is that it is a biological warning signal. Part of Sternbach's definition of pain illustrates this view (Sternbach, 1968):

> A harmful stimulus which signals current or impending tissue damage; a pattern of impulses which operate to protect the organism from harm.

There has been much thought about which pains are useful warnings. There is no doubt that survival depends upon the avoidance of bodily damage and the recognition of and action taken following injury. We tend to respond to all pains as biological warnings, including pains resulting from medical and nursing care such as surgery, blood taking, injections and endoscopy, even though these procedures are planned. The onset of pain is not always an adequate biological warning. Le Riche (1939) stated:

> As a matter of fact the majority of diseases even the most serious attack us without warning . . . when pain develops it is too late . . . pain is always a baleful gift.

There are many pains caused by disease and therapy which are useless as biological warnings, especially chronic pain syndromes such as causalgia and phantom pains.

Bonica (1982) made an important distinction between useful, useless and harmful pain. When harmful pain exists this means that pain *per se* is an emergency and must be relieved if the person is to avoid serious physiological complications or even death. The following graphic description of harmful pain was given by Bonica (1982):

Acute pain and reflex responses which develop in the postoperative period or after massive injury or burns have no useful function and if not promptly and effectively relieved produce progressively serious pathophysiological responses . . . excessive adrenergic activity, vagal inhibition and skeletal muscle spasm.

In addition, Bonica stated that:

Central sympathetic stimulation induced by anxiety causes pulmonary complications, marked inhibition of gastro-intestinal and genito-urinary activity with consequent ileus and oliguria; marked increase in the work load of the heart and excessive increase in the metabolism and oxygen consumption.

He mentioned specific pains including the pain of severe acute pancreatitis, biliary and renal colic which give rise to reflex spasm of abdominal and chest wall and hence provoke hypoventilation 'which unless promptly corrected may progress to death' (Bonica, 1982).

Other examples of harmful pain include postmyocardial infarction pain in which sympathetic overactivity can increase the discrepancy between myocardial oxygen supply and the demand for oxygen, and consequently increase the size of the infarct and the risk of death (Bonica, 1980).

The classification of pain as useful, useless and harmful does not mean that only harmful pain should be relieved, but that harmful pain is an emergency. Useless pain should also be relieved if humanly possible, and useful pain once recognized or even anticipated should be relieved if the sufferer so wishes.

Social meaning

The word 'meaning' in this context is a synonym of 'consequence'. It is not meant to convey the purpose of pain, as in philosophical and biological meaning, but rather to answer the question: what does it mean to have pain? What are the possible psychosocial consequences of having pain? If we reconsider Copp's categories of pain, i.e. life pain, disease-associated pain, therapy-initiated pain, nursing care-initiated pain, research-related pain and pain associated with the patient's decision to forgo treatment (Copp, 1985), it will be obvious that the likely psychosocial meanings will differ according to the circumstances.

Wall (1989a) made the interesting suggestion that pain is akin to a need state such as hunger and thirst, which demands action. Certainly the response of a person to pain leads to action at many levels, including thinking through their feelings and understanding of the meaning of pain, and changing and adapting their behaviour at physical and social levels. The disrupton of ongoing behaviour may range from the transient and minimal to the permanent and total change of lifestyle, depending on the nature of the pain and the circumstances of the sufferer. Table 9 summarizes the typical social consequences of pain.

Table 9. Social consequences of pain.

Search for a cause
Search for help
Disruption of ongoing behaviour
Disruption of lifestyle

Chronic pain: abdication of social responsibilities; interaction only in the sick role; isolation

Behavioural expressions of relief or recovery from pain
   Search for quietness and solitude
   Prolonged sleep
   Minimal movement
   Temporary antisocial behaviour

A brief pain such as a stubbed toe or an injection may merely provoke an orienting response, whereas a chronic intractable pain may result in the person retiring from work or ceasing any or all of the activities that were previously enjoyed.

The potential for pain to result in isolation was discussed in Chapter 2. Perhaps the most damaging consequence of persistent pain is the negative effect it may have upon the personality of the sufferer. Anger, depression, irritability and guilt can erode feelings of self-worth and corrode relationships with friends and family. Alternatively, such pains can have positive consequences—a search for others who are similarly afflicted, the setting up of self-help groups, learning to be active and to live well despite the pain. Bonica (1990) stated that chronic pain is associated with significant physical and social dysfunction. Romano *et al* (1992) used a chronic illness problem inventory (CIPI) (Kames *et al*, 1984) as a measure of dysfunction in chronic pain patients. This is a 65 item, self-report questionnaire and includes the following categories: social activity, contact with family and friends, employment, sleep, eating, marital difficulty, marital overprotection, finances, medications, cognitive activity, physical appearance, body deterioration, sex, assertion, medical interaction and non-married relationships. Tait *et al* (1990) described a specific pain disability index.

SELF-KNOWLEDGE ABOUT PAIN

People in pain are alone and vulnerable to the responses of those from whom they seek help and compassion. It is a tall order to attempt to look at our own fears, myths and prejudices honestly; but without some understanding of ourselves we risk misinterpreting the experience of others, and when faced by the distress of someone in pain we are in danger of spending more energy defending ourselves than helping them. Autton (1986) wrote: 'Patients in pain are apt to unmask the emotional and spiritual inadequacies of those striving to minister to them'. It is not possible to be alongside someone in pain and at the same time to be running away. Like the pain sufferer, we too will have culturally and personally developed meanings of pain. They may be similar or dissimilar to those of the patient.

There are a number of ways in which we can help to clarify our beliefs about pain, in addition to self-scrutiny. One is to listen to patients, another is to read research findings and so compare our beliefs with those of other people. The questions we may ask ourselves are: do I agree with that meaning, or point of view? Is it difficult or easy to imagine myself reacting to pain in that way?

The study of medical humanities sounds an interesting and exciting way of enhancing self-knowledge, by the multiprofessional study of relevant novels, poems, plays, films and journals, under the guidance of a lecturer with a background in literature (Robb and Murray, 1992). How, for instance, do we feel about the poetic expression of pain cited at the beginning of this book, written by the twentieth-century Lebanese poet which proceeds:

> And could you keep your heart in wonder at the daily miracles of your life, your pain would seem no less wondrous than your joy.
> (Kahlil Gibran, *The Prophet*)

We might also learn from examining our sense of humour. Black humour tends to conceal and reveal our fears, including fear of pain. The fear and experience of back pain is a professional hazard.

Perhaps the most useful and beneficial attitude is that we should not be judgemental and should not attach labels of virtue or vice to the way in which a person in pain behaves, even when we find it incomprehensible.

Repeated confrontation with pain can result in nurses and doctors minimizing patients' experience. When descriptive vignettes of patients' suffering were compared, Lenburg *et al* (1970) found that nuns and teachers inferred most pain and nurses and doctors least. The balance and credence which observers put on non-verbal and verbal expressions of pain is complex. Past research found that nurses believed that physiological and non-verbal behaviours were better indices of pain than verbal reports (Johnson, 1977), possibly because they are less easily subject to what is termed 'motivated dissimulation' or deliberate pretence (Kraut, 1978). This attitude leads to a failure to recognize the extent of chronic pain (Teske *et al*, 1983) and to the current plea to believe first and foremost the patients' verbal description of their pain.

There are myths that develop in any profession. The medical and nursing professions have particular myths about the appropriate use of analgesics. One is that children do not experience pain in the same way as adults because of nervous system immaturity. This is not tenable, as it has been known at least since 1968 that children are not neurologically defective as far as pain is concerned (Swafford and Allen, 1968). Unfortunately, the wrong belief has resulted in the withholding of anaesthetic and analgesic from many children in pain. Eland (1985), in a study of hospitalized children aged 4–10 years in the USA, found that 66% of the children received no analgesic for the relief of pain. Eland and Anderson (1977) compared analgesic doses received by 18 adults with those given to 18 children who had identical diagnoses and surgical procedures. The adults received 372 doses of narcotics and 299 doses of non-narcotics analgesics, whereas the children received 11 doses of narcotics and 13 of non-narcotic analgesics.

Research findings and observations of children's responses to pain leave us with no excuse whatsoever for minimizing or ignoring their suffering.

Other myths concern an exaggerated fear of addiction and of respiratory depression from narcotic drugs. The consequence has been that prescription of narcotic agents for severe pain and nursing administration of prescriptions *pro re nata* (p.r.n., as required) have been insufficient to relieve distress (Marks and Sachar, 1973). Porter and Jick (1980) in a survey of 12 000 adults and children found that addiction was rare in patients treated with narcotic drugs. Some patients are labelled as addicted when they demand injections and 'clockwatch' anxiously.

Such patients typically have gained inadequate analgesia from their current regimen and have experienced long delays in the administration of drugs. They are not demanding narcotics to gain psychological effects but to be relieved of pain (Twycross, 1984). This situation can arise for those with acute postoperative pain as well as for those with chronic pain.

Narcotic drugs do cause respiratory depression but severe pain is a powerful respiratory stimulant, so it is usually possible to achieve pain relief without dangerous compromise of respiration (Twycross, 1984). Walsh *et al* (1981) found that clinically important respiratory depression rarely occurred in patients with severe pain due to malignant disease, even when they received large doses of morphine.

There are other beliefs which may be held by nurses that can lead to the ignoring or minimizing of patients' pain and the omission of pain relief measures. These include the belief that people who laugh, talk and sleep cannot be in pain. A permanent solemn and miserable expression is thus demanded, if these attitudes are perceived by the patient.

Some facts about pain that may counteract past and present prejudices are listed in Table 10. Myths and misconceptions about the pain experienced by children (Gillies, 1993) and adults (Closs *et al*, 1993) still result in the underestimation and undertreatment of pain.

In summary, knowledge about the biological basis of pain, the potential experiences of people in pain, plus reflection on our beliefs and prejudices, may enhance nursing professional skill.

Table 10. Some facts about pain.

- Pain is not predictable from its cause or lack of cause
- Lack of a physical diagnosis does not justify psychiatric labelling (Wall, 1986)
- Children and mentally handicapped people do not feel less pain than adults (Swafford and Allen, 1968)
- Acute and chronic pain do not provoke the same responses
- Stoicism is not a virtue (though some patients may regard it as such)
- A high pain threshold is not a virtue, neither is a high pain tolerance
- Medication is not the only pain relief agent which works
- Narcotics used for pain relief rarely cause addiction (Porter and Jick, 1980)
- Narcotics used to relieve severe pain rarely depress respiration to a dangerous level (Twycross,.1984)
- *Pro re nata* administration of analgesic does not lead to less side-effects than regular administration (Editorial, 1978)
- The same doses of drug will not be effective for all patients
- People in pain can laugh, talk and sleep

REFERENCES

Autton N (1986) *Pain—An Exploration*, p 118. London: Darton, Longman & Todd.

Baken D (1968) *Disease, Pain and Sacrifice: Towards a Psychology of Suffering*. Boston: Beacon.

Bischoff A (1979) Congenital insensitivity to pain with anhidrosis. A morphological study of sural nerve and cutaneous receptors in the human prepuce. In Bonica JJ, Liebeskind JC & Albe-Ferrard DG (eds) *Advances in Pain Research and Therapy*, 3rd edn, pp 53–65. New York: Raven Press.

Blendis LM (1989) Abdominal Pain. In Wall P & Melzack R (eds.) *Textbook of Pain*, 2nd edn, Ch 32. Edinburgh: Churchill Livingstone.

Bonica JJ (1980) Introduction. *Pain* 58: 1–17.

Bonica JJ (1982) Introduction—Narcotic analgesics in the treatment of cancer and post-operative pain. Symposium Proceedings, Stockholm, Nov 12–14, 1980. *Acta Anaesthesioligica Scandinavica* 26 (supplement 74): 5–10.

Bonica JJ (1990) General considerations of pain in the low back, hips and lower extremities. In Bonica JJ (ed.) *The Management of Pain*, 2nd edn, vol. 2. Philadelphia: Lea and Febiger.

Brown WA (1968) Post amputation phantom limb pain. *Diseases of the Nervous System* 29: 301–306.

Carpenito LJ (1983) *Nursing diagnoses. Application to clinical practice*. Philadelphia: JB Lippincott.

Cassel EJ (1982) The nature of suffering and the goals of medicine. *New England Journal of Medicine* 306 (11): 639–645.

Cervero F (1987) Visceral pain. Fifth World Congress on Pain of the International Association for the Study of Pain. *Pain* (supplement 4) 51–54.

Closs SJ, Fairclough HL, Tierney AJ & Currie CT (1993) Pain in Elderly othopaedic patients. *Journal of Clinical Nursing* 2: 41–45.

Copp LA (1974) The spectrum of suffering. *American Journal of Nursing* 74 (3): 491–495.

Copp LA (1985) Pain ethics and the negotiation of values. In Copp LA (ed.) *Perspectives on Pain. Recent Advances in Nursing*. Edinburgh: Churchill Livingstone.

Cousins M (1989) Acute and postoperative pain. In Wall PD & Melzack R (eds) *Textbook of Pain*, 2nd edn, Ch. 18. Edinburgh: Churchill Livingstone.

Degenaar JJ (1979) Some philosophical considerations on Pain. *Pain* 7: 281–304.

Descartes R (1644) *L'Homme. Lectures on the history of physiology during the 16th, 17th & 18th centuries* (translated by Foster M). Cambridge University Press.

Diamond AW & Coniam SW (1991) *The Management of Chronic Pain*, pp 129–133. Oxford: Oxford University Press.

Domzal T, Szczudlik A, Kwasucki J, Zaleska B & Lypka A (1983) Plasma cortisol concentrations in patients with different circadian pain rhythms. *Pain* 17: 67–70.

Dubuisson D (1989) Nerve root damage and arachnoiditis. In Wall P & Melzack R (eds) *Textbook of Pain*, 2nd edn, Ch. 39. Edinburgh: Churchill Livingstone.

Dubuisson D & Melzack R (1976) Classification of clinical pain descriptions by multiple group discriminant analysis. *Experimental Neurology* 51: 480.

Editorial (1978) Postoperative pain. *British Medical Journal* 8: 517–518.
Eland JM & Anderson JE (1977) The experience of pain in children. In Jacox A (ed.) *Pain: A Sourcebook for Nurses and Other Health Professionals*. Boston: Little, Brown.
Eland JM (1985) The role of the nurse in children's pain. In Copp LA (ed.) *Perspectives on Pain: Recent Advances in Nursing*, 11, Ch. 3. Edinburgh: Churchill Livingstone.
Fields HL & Basbaum AI (1984) Endogenous pain control mechanism. In Wall PD & Melzack R (eds) *Textbook of Pain*, Ch 11, 1. Edinburgh: Churchill Livingstone.
Fish D, Twinn S & Purr B (1991) Promoting Reflection: Improving the Supervision of Practice in Health Visiting and Initial Teacher Training. HELPP Report No. 2. London: West London Press: West London Institute of Higher Education.
Gillies ML (1993) Post-operative pain in children: A review of the literature. *Journal of Clinic Nursing* 2: 5–10.
Glyn C (1987) Intractable pain: a problem identification and solving exercise. *Hospital Update* 13 (1): 44–54.
Glyn CL, Lloyd JW & Folkards S (1976) The diurnal variation in perception of pain. *Proceedings of the Royal Society of Medicine* 69: 369–372.
Head H & Sherrin J (1905) The consequences of injury to the peripheral nerves of man. *Brain* 28: 116.
Hebb DO (1949) *The Organisation of Behaviour*. Chichester: Wiley.
Holm K, Cohen F, Dudas S, Medema PG & Allen BL (1989) Effects of personal pain experience on pain assessment. Image: *Journal of Nursing Scholarship* 21 (2): 72–75.
Illich I (1976) *Limits to Medicine. Medical Nemesis: The Exploration of Health*, pp 151–155. Harmondsworth: Penguin.
International Association for the Study of Pain Sub-committee on Taxonomy (1979) Pain terms: a list with definitions and notes on usage. *Pain* 6: 249–252.
Jensen TS & Rasmussen P (1984) Amputation. In Wall PD & Melzack R (eds) *Textbook of Pain*, pp 402–412. Edinburgh: Churchill Livingstone.
Jensen TS & Rasmussen P (1989) Phantom pain and related phenomena after amputation. In Wall PD & Melzack R (eds) *Textbook of Pain*, 2nd edn, pp 508–521. Edinburgh: Churchill Livingstone.
Johnson M (1977) Assessment of clinical pain. In Jacox AK (ed.) *Pain: A Sourcebook for Nurses and Other Health Professionals*, pp 139–166. Boston: Little, Brown.
Kames LD, Naliboff BD, Heinrich RL & Schag CC (1984) The chronic illness problem inventory: problem oriented psychosocial assessment of patients with chronic illness. *International Journal of Psychiatric Medicine* 14: 65–75.
Kraut RE (1978) Verbal and nonverbal cues in the perception of lying. *Journal of Personal and Social Psychology* 36: 380–391.
Lenburg CB, Glass HP & Davitz LJ (1970) Pain in relation to the stage of the patient's illness and occupation of the perceiver. *Nursing Research* 19: 392–398.
Le Resche L (1982) Facial behaviour in pain: a study of candid photographs. *Journal of Nonverbal Behaviour* 7: 46.

Le Riche R (1939) *The Surgery of Pain* (translated and edited by Young A). Baltimore: Williams & Wilkins.

Le Shan L (1964) The world of the patient in severe pain of long duration. *Journal of Chronic Diseases* 17: 119–126.

Malliani A, Pagani M & Lombardi F (1984) Visceral versus somatic mechanisms. In Wall PD & Melzack R (eds). *Textbook of Pain*, Ch. 7. Edinburgh: Churchill Livingstone.

Marks RM & Sachar EJ (1973) Undertreatment of medical inpatients with narcotic analgesia. *Annals of International Medicine* 78: 173.

McCaffery M (1972) *Nursing Management of the Person in Pain*. Philadelphia: JB Lippincott.

Melzack R (1973) *The Puzzle of Pain*. Harmondsworth: Penguin.

Melzack R (1975) The McGill pain questionnaire: major properties and scoring methods. *Pain* 1 277–299.

Melzack R (1990) John J Bonica Distinguished Lecture. The Gate Control Theory 25 years later: new perspectives on phantom limb pain. *Pain* (supplement 5) 254.

Melzack R (1981) Current concepts of pain. In Saunders C, Summers DH & Teller N (eds) *Hospice: The Living Idea*. London: Edward Arnold.

Melzack R & Casey KL (1968) Sensory motivational and central control determinants of pain. A new conceptual model. In Kenshalo DR (ed.) *The Skin Senses*, pp 423–439. Springfield: CC Thomas.

Melzack R & Loeser JD (1978) Phantom body pain in paraplegics, evidence for a central 'pattern generating mechanism'. *Pain* 4: 195.

Melzack R & Wall PD (1965) Pain mechanisms. A new theory. *Science* 150: 971–979.

Melzack R & Wall PD (eds) (1984) Textbook of Pain. Edinburgh: Churchill Livingstone.

Melzack R, Wall PD & Ty TC (1982) Acute pain in an emergency clinic: latency of onset and descriptor pattern related to different injuries. *Pain* 14: 33–43.

Merskey H (1979) Pain Terms. *Pain* 6: 249–252.

Merskey H (1986) Classification of chronic pain: descriptions of chronic pain syndromes and definitions of pain terms. *Pain* (supplement 3) 1–225.

Messing RB & Lytle LD (1977) Serotonin containing neurons: their possible role in pain and analgesia. *Pain* 4: 1–21.

Price DB (1976) Phantom limb phenomenon in patients with leprosy. *Journal of Nervous and Mental Disease* 163: 108–116.

Popper K (1972) *The Logic of Scientific Discovery*. London: Hutchinson.

Porter J & Jick H (1980) Addiction rare in patients treated with narcotics. *New England Journal of Medicine* 302: 123.

Procacci P & Zoppi M (1984) Heart pain. In Wall PD & Melzack R (eds) *Textbook of Pain*, Ch 1. Edinburgh: Churchill Livingstone.

Procacci P & Zoppi M (1989) Heart pain. In Wall PD & Melzack R (eds) *Textbook of Pain*, 2nd edn, Ch 28. Edinburgh: Churchill Livingstone.

Procacci P, Della Corte M, Zoppi M & Maresca M (1974) Rhythmic changes of the cutaneous pain threshold in man. A general view. *Chronobiologia* 1: 77–96.

Rasmussen BK (1993) Migraine and tension-type headache in a general population: precipitating factors, female hormones, sleep pattern and relation to life style. *Pain* 53: 65–72.

Reading AE (1984) Testing pain mechanisms in persons in pain. In Wall
PD & Melzack R (eds) *Textbook of Pain*. Edinburgh: Churchill Livingstone.

Robb AJP & Murray R (1992) Medical humanities in nursing: thought provoking? *Journal of Advanced Nursing* **17**: 1182–1187.

Romano JM, Turner JA & Jensen MP (1992) The Chronic Illness Profile Inventory as a measure of dysfunction in chronic pain patients. *Pain* **49**: 71–75.

Royal College of Surgeons of England, College of Anaesthetists (1990) Commission for the provision of surgical services. *Report of the Working Party on
Pain After Surgery*, p 5.

Scadding JW (1989) Peripheral neuropathies. In Wall PD & Melzack R (eds)
Textbook of Pain, 2nd edn, Ch. 37. Edinburgh: Churchill Livingstone.

Sternbach RA (1963) Congenital insensitivity to pain: a critique. *Psychological
Bulletin* **60**: 252–264.

Sternbach RA (1968) *Pain, a Psychophysiological Analysis*. New York:
Academic Press.

Sternbach RA (1984) Acute versus chronic pain. In Wall PD & Melzack R (eds)
Textbook of Pain, Ch. 14. Edinburgh: Churchill Livingstone.

Stoddard FJ (1982) Coping with pain: a developmental approach to the
treatment of burned children. *American Journal of Psychiatry* **139**: 736–740.

Swafford LI & Allen D (1968) Pain relief in the pediatric patient. *Medical Clinics
of North America* **48**: 131–133.

Tait RC, Chibnall JT & Krause S (1990) The Pain Disability Index: psychometric
properties. *Pain* **40**: 171–182.

Teske K, Daut RL & Cleeland CS (1983) Relationships between nurses' observations and patients' selfreports of pain. *Pain* **16**: 289–296.

Twycross RG (1984) Narcotics. In Wall PD & Melzack R (eds) *Textbook of Pain*,
Ch. 3, s 2. Edinburgh: Churchill Livingstone.

Wall PD (1984) Introduction. In Wall PD & Melzack R (eds) *Textbook of Pain*, p 2.
Edinburgh: Churchill Livingstone.

Wall PD (1986) Causes of intractable pain. *Hospital Update* **12** (12): 969–974.

Wall PD (1989a) Introduction. In Wall P & Melzack R (eds) *Textbook of Pain*, 2nd
edn. Edinburgh: Churchill Livingstone.

Wall PD (1989b) The dorsal horn. In Wall P & Melzack R (eds) *Textbook of Pain*,
2nd edn, Ch. 5. Edinburgh: Churchill Livingstone.

Wall PD & Jones M (1991) *Defeating Pain. The War Against a Silent Epidemic*,
p 61. New York: Plenum.

Walsh TD, Baster R, Bowmank & Leber R (1981) High-dose morphine and
respiratory function in chronic cancern pain. *Pain* (supplement 1) 39.

Weddell G (1955) Somesthesis and the chemical senses. *Annual Review of
Psychology* **6**: 119.

Woolf CJ & Wall PD (1983) Endogenous opioid peptides and pain mechanisms:
a complex relationship. *Nature* **306**: 739–740.

4

Assessment of Pain

ASSESSMENT SKILLS

Assessment is a process by which we come to some conclusion about the nature of a problem. In the case of pain, it includes the recognition of pain, its likely cause, the context in which it is experienced and the resources available to deal with it.

Skill can be defined as knowledge combined with practical expertness (*Cassell's English Dictionary*). In Benner's terms the acquisition of skill could be expressed as the progression from novice to expert (Benner, 1984). Expertness is demonstrated by the person who can achieve skilled performance even in adverse circumstances. Skill therefore implies adaptability not rigidity of performance in achieving a goal.

The skills necessary for accurate assessment of pain are primarily those of communication and interpretation of both words and behaviour. Because pain is a subjective experience, 'a personal private sensation of hurt' (Sternbach, 1968), the transmission of information from the pain sufferer to other people is fraught with difficulty. The skills required of the nurse or other carer are of knowing how and what to hear, smell, touch and see, what interpretation to make, how to validate the pain experience with the patient and how to record and transmit this information to others. Nurses also have to be skilled in recognizing situations that may provoke pain. This skill is essential for the protection of the unconscious patient and any other person who is unable to communicate verbally (Table 1).

Decisions about goals and interventions cannot be made on the basis

Table 1. Assessment skills.

Decision-making
Observation
Validation
Interpretation
Recording and transmitting information
Goal setting

of the assessment of pain alone. The relationship of pain to other symptoms, diagnosis, treatment and lifestyle have also to be evaluated. The ability of the patient to cope and the nurse and the other carers to intervene, including the availability of environmental resources such as drugs, relaxation tape recordings and privacy, all need to be assessed (Table 2).

Table 2. Pain assessment aspects.

1. Pain:
   Nature, intensity and site
   Likely cause including medical diagnosis, treatment, nursing
   Precipitating factors and circumstances, e.g. movement, time of day, eating, drinking
2. Related and concurrent symptoms, e.g. nausea, anxiety, insomnia, breathlessness
3. Meaning and significance to the patient, i.e. purpose and consequences
4. Patient's desired goal
5. Resources:
   Patient's coping methods
   Nurse's knowledge and skills in using and teaching non-pharmacological methods of pain relief
   Medical and paramedical knowledge and skills in the use and provision of pharmacological and non-pharmacological methods of pain relief
   Availability of time, special equipment, drugs, privacy, etc.

DECISION-MAKING

The need to assess pain in people who have some illness seems obvious; but not all patients have pain, and many people with chronic non-malignant pain may not regard themselves (or be regarded by others) as ill. We have first of all to decide that pain assessment is an appropriate action, to believe that the person may have pain, and be committed to the act of assessment (see Nash *et al*, 1993). In many instances the point of assessment is to clarify the nature and extent of the pain experienced by the sick, or otherwise well, person such that logical and realistic goals may be agreed for the alleviation of the pain and appropriate methods of intervention selected and used.

Assessment has both advantages and disadvantages for patients, in that listening to patients and taking their pain seriously may in itself be therapeutic and reduce suffering. Conversely, encouraging a patient to examine and introspect their pain may increase that pain, particularly for the patient who has chronic pain and is using distraction as a method of reducing the experience of pain. In such circumstances it would be appropriate to ask the sufferers to decide if and when they wish to discuss and describe their pain. Ignoring and introspecting pain are mutually incompatible activities. The person who has severe pain will not be able or willing to spend long in assessing the pain—at least until some measure of relief is obtained. Where pain itself is an emergency which unrelieved may lead to further disease or death, as in some myocardial infarctions (Bonica, 1980), the assessment will need to be fast and accurate.

Who should do the assessment?

As pain is by its nature a subjective experience, the person in pain is the only one who can assess it accurately. This implies that wherever possible the patient should be the central assessor of the nature, intensity and meaning of pain. However, we are not infrequently faced by patients whose language we do not share, who are semiconscious or unconscious, or who are inarticulate (for instance babies or people with aphasia or deficient intellect). McCaffery's working definition that pain is 'whatever the experiencing person says it is and exists whenever he says it does' (McCaffery, 1972) is not applicable in the latter circumstances. Pain then has to be judged by the observer on indirect evidence. Interpretation of appearance, non-verbal behaviour, physiological status and circumstance are required. Belief that people in pain are *obviously* in pain can lead us to infer wrongly that there is no pain to assess.

It may be as well to admit in advance that the assessment of pain is an inexact art. People can pretend to have pain when they do not. McCaffery's response to this, which the authors endorse, is that it is better to err on the side of believing patients and not worry that occasionally we will be misled, than to start with an attitude of disbelief and force patients into exaggerated pain behaviour before they can convince us of their distress. One of the most terrible things we can do to people in pain is to refuse to believe them.

Sometimes the opposite problem occurs and the person genuinely does not experience pain in circumstances when we think they are bound to feel pain. This situation can arise because we wrongly believe that injury always results in pain. Our beliefs are challenged both by patients who have more pain than we expect and those who do not have pain when we think it inevitable.

Probably a much more common scenario is the patient who initially refuses to admit having pain but who actually does have it. There are many possible reasons other than stoicism that can lead a person to keep pain secret. Sharing such information requires trust—what are we going to do with this knowledge? Does it mean that something new has gone wrong? Will it delay their discharge home? Why tell us if they think we cannot do anything about it? Also, in some cultures the admission of pain is shameful (Sargent, 1984).

Successful assessment of pain depends on the nurse, the patient and their relationship. The patient needs to know that the nurse can be trusted, that he or she cares and is skilled. The nurse needs to know what prejudices and myths he or she brings to the relationship as well as knowing how, what and when to assess. Many of these points are illustrated in the assessments described in the first two care studies on pages 145–152.

Decisions about assessment are summarized in Table 3. *Who* should do the assessing depends upon the status of the patient including their desires, competence and consciousness; and upon the membership and skills of the team of carers, such as the nurse, doctor, physiotherapist, etc. (see Table 5 on page 81). *What* should be assessed by the nurse includes the pain assessment aspects listed in Table 2. Almost invariably people in pain have additional problems which may be directly or indirectly related. Indeed, sometimes the presenting problem is not pain but (for example) lack of sleep, anxiety, inactivity, indigestion or constipation; see care study 3 on page 153. Seers (1987) investigated the anxiety as well as the pain of postoperative patients, and Closs (1992) studied their sleep and night-time pain. *How* the assessment is undertaken will partly depend upon the nature and potential cause of the pain, but includes observation, measurement, conversation and recording. Methods and tools of assessment are discussed in the following pages. *When* to assess depends upon many factors including the wishes of the patient, the severity of the pain and the method and timing of pain therapies. For example, assessment could be undertaken before and after the administration of analgesics, either at the time when the drug is expected to have maximum effect or when a repeat dose can be taken.

Table 3. Assessment decision-making.

Who should do the assessing?
What should they assess?
How should they assess?
When should the assessment take place?

OBSERVATION

Observation is the skill of watching and noticing. Included in the skill of observation are the abilities to listen and hear, to look and see, to touch and feel and to smell. In these ways we may observe physiological and non-verbal behaviour indicating pain. It is possible to increase this ability by learning what to observe. Generally we have a tendency to see what we expect to see, what confirms our hypotheses and what accords with our beliefs. This is a drawback when it leads us to fail to see and hear subtle but crucial differences in pain.

Observations range from those done at a distance, to enhanced observations using instruments. We can use our senses of hearing and sight to advantage from a distance. Almost all non-verbal behaviour associated with pain—the bodily postures, mobility, vocalizations and facial expressions—can be seen and heard while approaching a person who is potentially in pain. Some people may in fact behave more spontaneously if they are unaware of our concern. Others tone down their responses in public so that they do not distress us or other patients (Fagerhaugh and Strauss, 1977). What we observe will give us our first clues to the experience of pain. In addition, we can make measurements of pulse and blood pressure and concurrently observe the person.

There are limitations on the extent to which the physiological and behavioural responses can reliably indicate the presence of pain. Gross physiological changes alone are not adequate criteria for the diagnosis of acute or chronic pain. The human body has a limited repertoire of responses, such that the autonomic response to many stressors including fear, the anticipation of pain and the experience of pain may be indistinguishable. Heart rate, for instance, is the final common effector of responses to many influences, i.e. muscular exercise, digestion, posture, altitude, climate, noise, psychosensory activity, drugs and emotion. Vogt *et al* (1973) stated that heart rate should be used as an index of a particular physiological or psychological stress factor only if the simultaneous influence of all other factors is properly taken into account.

Another problem of interpretation arises from the fact that initial values affect the possibility for change; for example, a person with pre-existing hypertension or tachycardia has little leeway for increase in these parameters due to pain.

It would be wonderful if differences in autonomic or behavioural responses accurately reflected different types and intensities of pain, particularly when we aim to assess pain in those who are totally or partially inarticulate, such as the unconscious, those with mental disabilities, the newborn or those whose language we do not share, but as Houde (1982) stated, both behavioural and autonomic signs are unreliable indices of pain severity and may be absent in patients with chronic pain. It is therefore obvious that we have to be particularly vigilant about potential causes of pain in the above groups of people.

VALIDATION

Two things can lead us to validate our conclusions about the pain a person is suffering: one is that we think they may be in pain because of their medical or surgical condition or injury; the other is that they show physical or behavioural signs that may indicate pain. Validation involves direct communication with the person to verify and increase our understanding of their pain. 'Commune' and 'communication' are derived from the Latin *communis*, meaning 'common', and as Autton (1986) suggested, 'when we communicate we are trying to establish a "commonness" with someone'. Communication to validate the existence, nature, intensity and meaning of pain requires us to listen with understanding to spontaneous descriptions and ask whatever questions are appropriate to the particular circumstances. Communication about pain is not an easy process for the person in pain or for the person who wishes to understand. Crawford-Clark (1984) said that reports of pain are a 'noisy' source of information since they represent a complex sensory and emotional experience. Some people are much more adept at sharing their feelings and thoughts than others. We have therefore to consider ways in which we can help people to express their pain experience. A huge area of pain research has been devoted to the development of assessment tools which aim to enhance the person's verbal expression of their suffering so that they can convey in an overt way their subjective experience. We can provide the patient with selections of words, with body outlines and scales or a combination of all three. Many people have more than one site or type of pain, so a combination of assessment tools may be required to achieve comprehensive assessment.

Verbal description

Melzack (1981) suggested that there are four major classes of pain words: sensory, affective, evaluative and miscellaneous. The McGill–Melzack pain questionnaire (Melzack, 1975) contains examples of such words. This comprehensive tool has been widely used in research and to some extent in clinical practice, and a shortened format was published in 1987 (Melzack, 1987).

We aim to enable the person to use or choose their own words to describe their pain so that we do not put our words into their mouths and merely confirm our expectations. McCaffery and Beebe (1989) suggested that we might help a patient who finds the pain indescribable by asking: 'What would you do to me to have me feel the pain you have?' For an amputee to say that he would twist a knife between our toes, would leave us in no doubt of the nature of his pain.

Discussion or history-taking can help us to clarify the likely causes and precipitating factors, the behaviours, movements and times when the pain is worst, and the ways in which the person copes with or attempts to reduce the pain. Detailed verbal description is inappropriate when pain needs immediate relief. Some timid patients will persevere with assessment conversation even though they wish we would go away or intervene; bolder patients may interrupt and tell us their need.

Children may have particular difficulty in expressing pain. They may not use the word 'pain', but 'hurt' or 'owie' (Eland and Anderson, 1977) or some more idiosyncratic term. Their parents may be essential assessors and interpreters, although parents tend to think that nurses automatically know when their child is in pain and the parents' personal distress can result in failure to recognize their own child's hurt. Eland (1985) found that children can tell the truth about their pain if they are given appropriate ways to express their hurt. However, they may not admit to pain if they associate the admission of pain with the infliction of more pain (by intramuscular injections), and Eland found that intramuscular injections are classed by most children as the worst hurt they experienced in hospital. Also, it is possible that some children may not recognize their discomforting symptoms as pain or hurt if the onset is insidious—accepting the status quo as normal or inevitable. Eland (1985) described one such child, a 13-year-old with advanced carcinoma who, when given regular analgesics, stated:

> 'I really did not think I hurt until you took it [the pain] away. Now I really feel great and I sleep a lot better. I had kind of forgotten what it was like not to hurt.'

Scaling techniques

There will never be an instrument that will perfectly transduce subjective pain into an objective form in the way that a thermometer measures temperature, though some researchers have sought it; for example, Chen and Chapman (1980) investigated the amplitude of electrical potentials recorded from the scalp. However, the intensity of pain has been measured fairly successfully using psychophysical scales. Simple lines or elaborated visual scales such as Hayward's pain thermometer (Hayward, 1975) and Bourbonnais's pain rule (Bourbonnais, 1981) are most commonly used in nursing evaluation of pain intensity (Figure 1).

The ability being tested is a complex one. Hallsten (1980) in his discussion of the puzzle of ratio scaling described the task which the subject or patient is asked to perform, i.e. to compare some internal state with an external numbered and symbolically worded scale. He stated:

> Not only do we not know what the person is doing when making the comparison, but neither do we know what he is measuring (in his internal milieu) . . . yet it is a task which subjects are willing to undertake, do not regard as an unreasonable request, and furthermore provides data which are reasonably consistent with the experimenter's expectations.

A line or visual analogue scale may be divided into equal divisions and numbered, e.g. from 0 to 10, or only numbered at the ends. Anchor words at either end are usual, e.g. 'no pain' (0) to 'unbearable', 'excruciating' or 'worst pain' (10). Words may be attached at set intervals, e.g. 'none', 'slight', 'moderate' and 'severe' (Houde, 1982), or 'no pain', 'just noticeable', 'weak', 'mild', 'moderate', 'strong', 'severe' and 'excruciating' (Tursky, 1976); or numbers may have behavioural consequences attached (Linton and Götestam, 1983). Finally, the scale

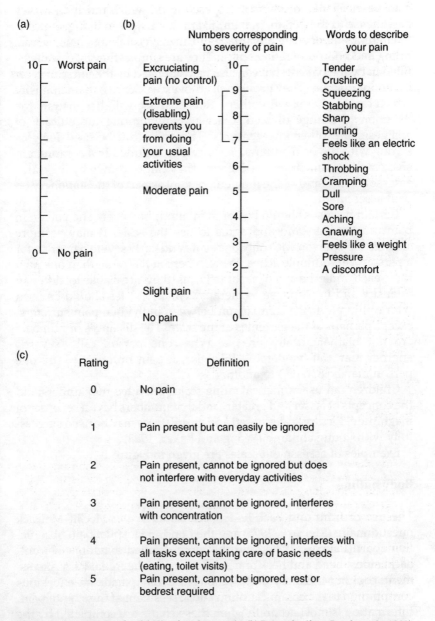

Figure 1. *Assessment scales: (a) Visual analogue scale. (b) Pain ruler (from Bourbonnais, 1981). The patient is instructed to match the words that apply to the pain with a number on the ruler which corresponds to the severity of the pain, then draw an arrow from the word to the number, or tell the nurse. (c) Verbal rating scale (from Linton and Göteskam, 1983).* Reproduced with permission.

may be horizontal or vertical, depending on which direction makes most sense to the person in pain. Examples are given in Figure 1.

There are enormous advantages in using visual analogue, verbal rating and numerical rating scales. They are simple; they can ideally be filled in by the patient, but can also be completed by the nurse or carer under instruction. They provide clear, overt evidence of pain intensity which can be shared with others. Repeated use will demonstrate the direction of change of pain, crucial for monitoring the efficacy of analgesic and other interventions. The scales can be used for goal setting with the pain sufferer. They can be included in a comprehensive pain assessment, or used alone. They can be drawn by the nurse assessor on the spur of the moment, or kept as part of the stationery on pain assessment.

Certain provisos should be borne in mind, however. The person in pain must understand and agree to use the scale. It may be more suitable for a person with only one acute and fairly severe pain than for a person with multiple aches. When a person has more than one pain then each must be rated separately, as they are liable to differ in intensity and in response to therapy. Finally, scales should be used with caution to make comparison between individual pain sufferers, except perhaps at the extremes of the scale. The distances or numbers are not mathematically precise. What one person calls 'severe', another may call 'moderate'. Likewise, a pain numbered 7 by one person may be 8, 6 or 5 to another.

Children can use numerical rating scales provided they understand the concepts of lesser and greater, and that numbers have a set order of magnitude. Picture scales of sad and happy faces may be used successfully with young children (Wong and Baker, 1988).

Examples of assessment scales are given in Figure 1.

Body outline

The use of front and back body outlines as in the McGill–Melzack questionnaire (Melzack, 1975) and the London Hospital pain observation chart (Raiman, 1986), and the more detailed diagrams of front, back, sides, head and neck and soles of feet in the Initial Pain Assessment Tool of McCaffery and Beebe (1989), have made an enormous contribution to the communication and assessment of the sites of pain. Information is most accurate when these charts are completed by the pain sufferer, but they can be filled in by the nurse under the instruction of the patient if necessary. The person in pain does not need to know anatomical terms but merely shades in the parts of the body that hurt, thus clarifying the extent of pains and the different sites of pain. The only drawback is that the two-dimensional diagram cannot indicate whether the pain is superficial or deep. Each pain site can be assigned a number or letter and pain intensity and characteristics sought separately. In this way the differential response of each pain can be monitored.

Body outlines are also helpful in assessing children's pain. Eland's colour tool uses body outlines and eight coloured crayons (Eland, 1985). The child is asked to select the four colours which represent severe, middling, little and no pain or hurt:

1. the event which the child said hurt most, representing severe pain;
2. not quite as much as the event which the child said hurt most, so representing middle pain;
3. the colour which is like 'hurts a little', representing little hurt, and
4. the colour which is like 'no hurt at all'.

This assessment tool has been used by many researchers and is said to be a reliable and valid instrument (Eland, 1985).

INTERPRETATION

Interpretation skills are most needed when we cannot communicate verbally with the person in pain and have to rely on our judgement of the possible pain-provoking circumstances and the physiological and non-verbal behaviours which we observe. It may be better to find an interpreter when attempting to assess the pain of a person whose language we do not share, than rely on our 'guesstimates'. If there is the time and opportunity to use an interpreter we can also agree some form of sign language with the pain sufferer to ensure that changes in pain can be communicated.

Babies—even premature babies (Johnston *et al*, 1993)—and young children are excellent non-verbal communicators of acute pain by facial expression, physiological response and vocalization. Williamson and Williamson (1983) suggested that circumcision pain response in unanaesthetized babies (i.e. without penile block) is similar to that of adults who are in extreme pain, if pain is judged by physiological response such as heart and respiratory rate increase. Izard *et al* (1980) described the facial expression of infants during medical procedures such as inoculation as 'brows down and together, nasal root broadened and bulged, eyes tightly closed, and the mouth angular and squarish'.

These expressions of pain were followed by anger expressions in which the eyes are open and staring. Haslam (1969) and Jay *et al* (1983) concluded from observations of overt distress caused by laboratory-induced pain and painful medical procedures, that the younger the child, the more pain seems to be experienced.

The group of patients for whom we need to be most vigilant in interpreting potentially painful situations are those who are unconscious or semiconscious. Whether or not they are aware of pain at the time, such people have lost the protective function of pain and the abilities to minimize bodily damage and express their pain. People who are paralysed are similarly at risk in those parts of the body that have lost sensation and movement. The frequent postural changes triggered by discomfort have to be carried out for the unconscious or taught as a deliberate act to the paralysed if ligaments, joints and muscles are to be saved from damage. Thoughtful assessment of bodily posture and alignment as well as any pain-provoking procedure may hasten the recovery of patients whose condition is reversible and reduce the likelihood of complications in all.

RECORDING AND TRANSMITTING INFORMATION

As members of a team of carers it is crucial that we can share our knowledge of the patients' pain with doctors, physiotherapists and anyone else involved in the alleviation of pain, or help the patient to do so directly. Many of the assessment tools are excellent for this purpose because they put into an overt form the subjective experience of the patient. They transform private, inaccessible knowledge into a publicly accessible format. The exact method chosen to record patients' pain should be appropriate to the type and amount of information, above all unambiguous and preferably concise. The creative use of published pain assessment formats such as that of McCaffery and Beebe (1989) or the London Hospital pain observation chart (Raiman, 1986) (Figure 2), both designed for initial and ongoing assessment and evaluation of pain interventions, would provide a comprehensive record. Nursing process care plans or SOAPE notes (Subjective, Objective, Assessment, Plan, Evaluation) may be inadequate as the sole record. Special pain assessment stationery may be designed to fulfil particular needs, or a pain scale added to existing charts. People in chronic or intermittent pain in the community can use diary formats such as the daily diary designed by McCaffery and Beebe (1989) or the London Hospital home diary (Raiman, 1986).

Somehow written documentation of pain acquires the status of proof which is not always accorded to oral statements. Recorded information may be added to by any and all members of the team of carers including the pain sufferer, and it provides the necessary legal documentation of care. Most importantly, it forms the basis for discussion of appropriate interventions and the resources available to the person in pain, the nurses, medical and paramedical staff, family and friends. Patients may benefit directly from using pain assessment tools in that some control is restored to them.

GOAL SETTING

The goal or outcome should be realistic. Hanks (1983) suggested that the goal of pain relief should not be confined simply to its effectiveness, but also related to the time of day and activity of the person. He suggested progressive goals for advanced cancer pain: firstly, to be free from pain at night; secondly, to be free from pain when at rest; and thirdly, to be free from pain on movement. The first two goals are almost always achievable, the third is more difficult.

Goal setting could logically be related to the category of pain. The obliteration of useful pain before arriving at a conclusion about its cause may possibly be counterproductive. The assessment of site, intensity, spread, precipitating factors, etc. may be helpful to diagnosis. This decision is, however, likely to be a joint medical and nursing one. Analgesia does not necessarily mask clinical signs.

Useless pain, including most postoperative pain and chronic pain, where the causes are iatrogenic or known, as well as any other tractable pain, should logically be completely relieved, if the person in pain so wishes and this goal can be achieved. Patients regard unrelieved postoperative pain as highly stressful (Volicier and Bohannon, 1975) and a serious complication (McConnell, 1983). Sofaer (1984) found that a higher percentage of patients wanted complete relief than did the nurses. Some patients use their pain to self-monitor postoperative progress, and although the eventual expected outcome is 'no pain' they prefer to tolerate moderate or mild pain than to obliterate the pain with analgesics (Fordham, 1985).

The goal for harmful or potentially harmful pain should be immediate reduction or elimination if the dangerous sequelae are to be avoided (Bonica, 1982). This assessment and decision is likely to be a

The London Hospital
PAIN OBSERVATION CHART

This chart records where a patient's pain is and how bad it is, by the nurse asking the patient at regular intervals. If analgesics are being given regularly, make an observation *with* each dose and another *half-way between* each dose. If analgesics are given only 'as required', observe 2-hourly. When the observations are stable and the patient is comfortable, any regular time interval between observations may be chosen.

TO USE THIS CHART ask the patient to mark all his or her pains on the body diagram below. Label each site of pain with a letter (i.e., A, B, C, etc.).

Then at each observation time ask the patient to assess:

1. The pain in each separate site since the last observation. Use the scale above the body diagram, and enter the number or letter in the appropriate column.
2. The pain overall since the last observation. Use the same scale and enter in column marked OVERALL.

Next, record what has been done to relieve pain:

3. Note any analgesic given since the last observation stating name, dose, route, and time given.
4. Tick any other nursing care or action taken to ease pain.

Finally, note any comment on pain from patient or nurse (use the back of the chart as well, if necessary) and initial the record.

DATE...

SHEET NUMBER.....................

TIME	PAIN RATING								OVER-ALL
	BY SITES								
	A	B	C	D	E	F	G	H	

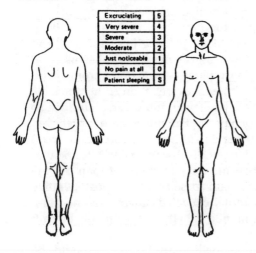

Excruciating	5
Very severe	4
Severe	3
Moderate	2
Just noticeable	1
No pain at all	0
Patient sleeping	S

Figure 2. *The London Hospital pain observation chart* (from Raiman, 1986).

PATIENT
IDENTIFICATION
LABEL

ANALGESIC GIVEN (Name, dose, route, time)	Lifting	Turning	Massage	Distracting activities	Position change*	Additional aids	Other	COMMENTS FROM PATIENTS AND/OR STAFF	Initials

MEASURES TO RELIEVE PAIN   Specify where starred

medical one, with the nurse as a secondary assessor and evaluator. Realistic goal setting for many chronic, intractable, phantom and intermittent pains is far from straightforward. Multidisciplinary assessment and discussion of available interventions and likely outcomes are essential to realistic goal setting with and for these persons (Glyn, 1987).

The reassessment of pain is alternatively termed evaluation. Reassessment is necessary for all but the most transitory pains. These repeated assessments may reveal a clearer picture if carried out by the same person. However, it is crucial that the same tool is used for evaluation as was used for the initial assessment if accurate monitoring of change is to be achieved.

In conclusion, the act of pain assessment depends upon the knowledge and skills of the nurse and the pain sufferer and their ability to achieve some degree of mutuality or commonness. There are stages in assessment which have to be judged creatively according to the nature and circumstances of the person's pain. A quick initial assessment followed by intervention, then a longer history-taking and more thorough assessment, plus continuing evaluation may be most appropriate for severe acute pain. A detailed history and assessment of pain may be possible as an initial step for chronic pain. Whatever the method chosen to assess pain, the desired outcome is to agree a goal for pain relief with the pain sufferer, if this is possible, and to make a decision about the interventions (or non-intervention) most likely to achieve that goal.

REFERENCES

Autton N (1986) *Pain: An Exploration*. London: Darton, Longman & Todd.
Benner P (1984) *From Novice to Expert. Excellence and Power in Clinical Nursing Practice*. Menlo Park: Addison-Wesley.
Bonica J (1980) Introduction to pain. *Pain* **58**: 1–17.
Bonica J (1982) Introduction: Narcotic analgesics in the treatment of cancer and post-operative pain. Symposium proceedings, Stockholm, Nov 12–14, 1980. *Acta Anaesthesiologica Scandinavica* (supplement 74) **26**: 5–10.
Bourbonnais F (1981) Pain assessment: development of a tool for the nurse and the patient. *Journal of Advanced Nursing* **6**: 277–282.
Chen ACN & Chapman CR (1980) Aspirin analgesia evaluated by event-related potentials in man: possible central action in pain. *Experimental Brain Research* **39**: 359–364.
Closs SJ (1992) *Surgical patients' experiences of sleep, night-time pain and analgesic provision*. PhD Thesis. Department of Nursing Studies, Edinburgh University.

Crawford-Clark W (1984) Applications of multidimensional scaling to problems in experimental and clinical pain. In Bromm B (ed.) *Pain Measurement in Man: Neurophysiological Correlates of Pain*, pp 349–369. Amsterdam: Elsevier.

Eland JM (1985) The role of the nurse in children's pain. In Copp LA (ed.) *Perspectives on Pain. Recent Advances in Nursing* 11. Edinburgh: Churchill Livingstone.

Eland JM & Anderson JE (1977) The experience of pain in children. In Jacox A (ed.) *Pain: a Source Book for Nurses and Other Health Professionals*. Boston: Little, Brown.

Fagerhaugh SY & Strauss A (1977) *Politics of Pain Management: Staff Patient Interaction*. Menlo Park: Addison-Wesley.

Fordham M (1985) *Deconditioning and reconditioning following elective surgery*. Thesis (unpublished), London University.

Glyn C (1987) Intractable Pain. A problem identification and solving exercise. *Hospital Update* 13 (1): 44–54.

Hallsten L (1980) The puzzle of 0.7 and some other issues of ratio scaling. *Report 80*. Institute of Applied Psychology, University of Stockholm.

Hanks GW (1983) Management of symptoms in advanced cancer. *Update* 26 (10): 1691–1702.

Haslam DR (1969) Age and the perception of pain. *Psychosomatic Science* 15: 86.

Hayward J (1975) *Information a Prescription against Pain*. London: Royal College of Nursing.

Houde RW (1982) Methods for measuring clinical pain in humans. *Acta Anaesthesiologica Scandinavica* (supplement 74) 25–29.

Izard CE, Huebner RR, Risser D, McGinnes GG & Dougherty LM (1980) The young infant's ability to produce discrete emotion expressions. *Developmental Psychology* 16: 132.

Jay SM, Ozolins M, Eliot CH et al (1983) Assessment of children's distress during painful medical procedures. *Health Psychology* 2: 133–147.

Johnston CC, Stevens B, Craig KD & Granau RVE (1993) Developmental changes in pain expression in premature, full-term, two and four-month-old infants. *Pain* 52: 201–208.

Linton SJ & Götestam KG (1983) A clinical comparison of two pain-scales: correlation remembering chronic pain and measure of compliance. *Pain* 17: 57–65.

McCaffery M (1972) *Nursing Management of the Patient in Pain*. Philadelphia: JB Lippincott.

McCaffery M & Beebe A (1989) *Pain—Clinical Manual for Nursing Practice*. St Louis: CV Mosby.

McConnell EA (1983) After surgery: how you can avoid the obvious . . . and the not so obvious hazards. *Nursing (US)* 13 (3): 8–15.

Melzack R (1975) The McGill pain questionnaire: major properties and scoring methods. *Pain* 1: 277–299.

Melzack R (1981) Current concepts of pain. In Saunders C, Summers DH & Teller N (eds) *Hospice: The Living Idea*. London: Edward Arnold.

Melzack R (1987) The short-form McGill pain questionnaire. *Pain* 30: 191–197.

Nash R, Edwards H & Nebauer M (1993) Effects of attitudes, subjective norms and perceived control on nurses' intention to assess patients' pain. *Journal of Advanced Nursing* 18: 941–947.

Raiman J (1986) Towards understanding pain and planning for relief. *Nursing* 11: 411–423.

Sargent C (1984) Between death and shame: dimensions of pain in Bariba culture. *Social Science and Medicine* 19 (12): 1299–1304.

Seers K (1987) *Pain, anxiety and recovery in patients undergoing surgery.* PhD thesis (unpublished), London University.

Sofaer B (1984) *The effect of focused education for nursing teams on post-operative pain of patients.* Thesis (unpublished), Edinburgh University.

Sternbach RA (1968) *Pain, A Psychophysiological Analysis.* New York: Academic Press.

Tursky B (1976) The development of a pain perception profile: a psychological approach. In Weisenberg M & Tursky B (eds) *New Perspectives in Therapy and Research.* New York: Plenum Press.

Vogt JJ, Meyer-Schwertz MT & Foehr R (1973) Motor, thermal and sensory factors in heartrate variation. A methodology for indirect estimation of intermittent muscular work and environmental heat loads. *Ergonomics* 16: 45–60.

Volicier BJ & Bohannon MW (1975) A hospital stress rating scale. *Nursing Research* 24 (5): 352–359.

Williamson PS & Williamson ML (1983) Physiologic stress reduction by a local anaesthetic during newborn circumcision. *Pediatrics* 71: 36–40.

Wong DL & Baker CM (1988) Pain in children: comparison of assessment scales. *Pediatric Nursing* 14: 9–17.

5

Principles of Effective Pain Management

The nursing care of people in pain involves two distinct but inter-
twined skills—management skills and technical skills in the use of
pharmacological and non-pharmacological therapies. It is difficult to
produce a definitive list of management skills as these are diffuse and
legion, but it is possible to attempt to define the domains of nursing
management. These include management of people and their relationships, i.e. self, patient, family and friends of patient, and colleagues;
and management of environments, i.e. work, home, leisure, hospital
(Table 1).

Table 1. Domains of
nursing management.

Self
Person in pain
Team of carers
Environment

Management skills are acquired by experience and require models
(expert nurses), instances, reflection, discussion and outcome investigation (Benner, 1984). Appropriate management depends upon the
role of the nurse in relationship to others and to the specific situation in
which pain occurs.

Pain control techniques that a nurse may utilize to help the person in pain include pharmacological methods, touch therapies and verbal interventions. Teaching and facilitation of patient-controlled methods of coping with pain involve both management and technical skills.

It is evident that nurses are faced with new dilemmas and decisions concerning their role in the care of people in pain as a result of both scientific progress and social change. In the first chapter we noted that understanding of the phenomenon of pain is increasing apace. This developing knowledge about pain is accompanied by changing ideas about pain management and control techniques. Concomitant with these changes, the role of the nurse and the expectations of patients are evolving. This chapter and those that follow discuss the issues that face nurses in the changing context in which they work (Table 2). This chapter discusses principles of pain management including ethical considerations; Chapter 6 discusses pharmacological management, Chapter 7 non-pharmacological management and Chapter 8 nursing interventions in terms of the roles adopted by nurses, patients, and other carers.

Table 2. Nursing issues in the management of pain.

Principles of effective pain management
Ethical considerations
Techniques of pain control

GENERAL PRINCIPLES OF PAIN MANAGEMENT

Sometimes pain relief is straightforward and easily effected. In other situations pain presents a challenge to the wide range of expertise of the various members of the health-care team. However, some general principles apply to all pain situations. Characteristics of good management are listed in Table 3.

One factor which should be borne in mind in managing pain is that covert and overt inequalities of power exist between professional

Table 3. Characteristics of good management.

1. Handles with skill, care and consideration
2. Is participative and/or consultative
3. Implies adaptation and acknowledges the possibility of continuing difficulty

carers and between carers and patients. For example, the nurse's knowledge of specific techniques for pain management as well as familiarity with the health services is a source of power. One hallmark of skilful nursing is an ability to help the person in pain without exploiting or abusing this unequal relationship and indeed to actively help to empower the patient. The principles of effective pain management are summarized in Table 4.

Table 4. Principles of effective pain management.

1. *Partnership* resulting from shared activities of the nurse and the person in pain
2. *Problem solving* beginning with the initial assessment and sustained through regular review and evaluation of treatment
3. *Individualized care* requiring an individualized approach
4. *Multidimensional management* enhanced when the multidimensional nature of pain is acknowledged
5. *Skilled companionship* (see Chapter 2) reducing the isolation engendered by pain

Partnership in pain

Partnership entails helping patients to be as involved with their own care as they wish and are able to be (some patients may be paralysed or semiconscious, for instance). This empowerment has two aspects. First, patients must have the required information and tools to be involved; and second, they must be given the opportunity to negotiate whatever degree of involvement they want.

Working in partnership may take many forms, but in each situation the patient can define the amount of active and direct involvement wanted. Many patients happily leave decision-making to the 'experts'. Others wish to know the plans and the rationale behind decisions, but want the health professionals to take the primary responsibility. Still others want to be active participants, being given information to engage knowledgeably in decision-making and take part confidently in chosen interventions.

In the previous chapter, shared activity was suggested in the interplay between the nurse and the person in pain during the assessment phase. In relation to pain management this interplay is crucial. Both nurse and patient are committed to the shared goal of managed pain, and each offers unique knowledge and skills that will shape interventions. The aim of nursing is to bring together the knowledge and skill of pain interventions with the patient's unique experience.

In the context of enduring or severe pain, the personal relationship increases in importance. In fact, in one study, terminally ill people identified the 'interconnectedness' of nurse and patient as a strategy fostering and supporting hope. Non-involvement was reported to produce feelings of isolation which diminished hope (Vaillot, 1970; Herth, 1990).

Problem solving

Effective pain management rests on a systematic problem-solving approach that is familiarly known as the nursing process (Figure 1). During assessment, an understanding of a particular person's pain emerges from the objective and subjective data collected. The characteristics of pain and the problems created by it—functional, emotional, social and spiritual—are defined. These defined problems may then be arranged by the patient with the nurse and other carers in order of priority, so giving direction to subsequent phases of the process.

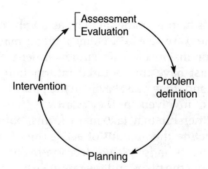

Shaped by the patient's priorities,
degree of involvement and choice
of interventions

Figure 1. *The nursing process.*

During the planning phase the nurse's and other carers' repertoire of pain therapies can be matched with the patient's problems; resources identified and realistic goals set. These goals often comprise improved function, such as being able to sleep through the night or walk to the shops. Implemented interventions include pharmacological and non-pharmacological treatments, education and counselling. The evaluation phase assesses the impact that interventions have had on both pain and any concomitant problems; this is a reassessment. The accuracy of evaluation may be enhanced by using the same methods and tools as the initial assessment (see Chapter 4), and may lead to a resetting of goals or selection of additional or alternative therapies.

Written nursing plans can be used to coordinate consistent care by the various care givers involved. They also enable the measurement of the effectiveness of nursing activities by documenting the clinical judgement and skill (or otherwise) of the nurse.

Individualized care

Effective pain management has at its foundation a shared or congruent understanding of the individual's experience of pain. It is clear that while pain is a universal phenomenon, the form it assumes is unique to the person who is experiencing it. The importance of this understanding cannot be overemphasized. If a mismatch evolves during the assessment phase, the nurse may develop inaccurate conclusions about the pain, and use approaches and offer interventions that do not address the problems that actually exist for the patient. For example, someone who interprets their pain as a sign of continued life, albeit unpleasant life, may resist measures to eliminate the pain, but be open to measures that minimize it to a level that allows them more independent functioning.

Pain management is also governed by the patient in so far as the nurse makes effective use of strategies used in the past by the person in pain to deal with their pain. Effective management involves not only sharing an understanding of the person's pain, but offering techniques that match their beliefs, resources and experiences. Therefore assessment—the definition of pain and the impact of that pain on the individual—is an activity that continues during the exploration, choice and administration of specific techniques of pain management. The patient's personal strategies give clues as to what may be acceptable for the nurse to suggest as non-pharmacological interventions, and how techniques may be offered that build on past experience. For example, an individual may have found in the past that resting quietly and trying to relax offers some relief; in which case, appropriate techniques may include deliberate deep muscle relaxation or positioning for maximum relaxation. In most circumstances success in pain management partly belongs to the person in pain, and partly to the carers.

Multidimensional management

The fact that the pain experience comprises several dimensions (sensory, emotional, behavioural) implies that it may be addressed simultaneously by a variety of means; and when several approaches are made, a synergistic effect may be brought about. For example, the dose of opioid analgesic required to manage a certain pain may be reduced when the person in pain is offered help to explore the meaning of their pain. Relaxation exercises may reduce muscle tension as well as anxiety and result in a decreased need for analgesics, as well as fostering a more effective response to other non-pharmacological interventions.

Pain teams have long acknowledged the importance of the variety of expertise multiprofessional teams bring to pain management. Distinctive activities of some members of the pain team are summarized in Table 5. Whilst each member offers a specific contribution, health-care professionals who are frequently involved with people in pain may share similar functions, especially in relation to emotional support. The person in pain, however, is consistently the integrating focus of everyone's activities.

Skilled companionship

Skilled companionship has been discussed in Chapter 2 and is fundamental to the nurse's potential contribution to effective pain management.

ETHICAL DIMENSIONS OF PAIN MANAGEMENT

The goal of nursing is to provide compassionate, effective and ethical care (see also Edwards, 1984; Whedon and Ferrell, 1991). Managing pain ethically requires the observance of human rights, and some human rights threatened in pain management are listed in Table 6.

Patient rights can only be claimed and respected if responsibilities are fulfilled by professional carers. The responsibilities of nurses and doctors and the rights of patients are not absolutely clear-cut, and agreed ethical behaviour is open to debate.

Autonomy

It can be argued that people in pain have the right to autonomy (self-governance). This implies that they should give *informed consent* to

Table 5. Contribution of members of the multiprofessional pain team.

Pain patient (if willing and able to participate)
Assesses and evaluates own pain and responses to pain relief
Helps professionals to understand the impact of pain on their feelings and
    lifestyle
Helps to set goals for desirable and realistic relief of pain and/or activity
    despite chronic pain
Participates in pain management

Doctor
Diagnoses the cause or lack of cause of the pain
Prescribes treatment, especially pharmacologic agents
Provides information about the pain and its treatment
Offers support, particularly through availability, information and a
    sympathetic relationship

Nurse
Helps the patient communicate what the pain means
Administers prescribed treatment
Offers non-pharmacologic interventions
Provides emotional support in the immediate situation
Helps the patient to:
    understand information
    share decision-making, if desired
    participate in management, if desired
Assists the patient in coping with pain

Social worker/counsellor
Provides long-term emotional support to patient and family
Works with patient to deal with the problems that arise related to pain

Physiotherapist
Assesses mechanical functioning
Prescribes physical therapies
Provides emotional support

Occupational therapist
Assesses activity achievements
Provides advice on activities and aids for living

Psychologist
Assesses psychological status
Offers psychotherapeutic interventions
Offers behaviour therapy where appropriate

Spiritual leader (chaplain, priest, rabbi, imam)
Offers spiritual interpretation appropriate to the spiritual beliefs of the
    patient
Offers emotional and cultural support

Family, friends and neighbours
Provide practical and emotional support

Table 6. Human rights important in
pain management.

Autonomy
Protection from unnecessary pain
Freedom from unwanted pain
Privacy

---

any therapeutic intervention. Informed consent requires that the person making the decision does so on the basis of the best available information. Failure to share information with patients and to allow patients to take their own decisions if they so wish about the choice of pain intervention is sometimes justified by carers on the grounds that the carers have the right, or in some circumstances the duty, to decide what is best for the sick. This attitude of paternalism has a long and honourable history but is less acceptable in the present day. This change in the relationship between patients and professionals is a reflection of societal change. Authority figures in many spheres of life, including politics, education, religion and health care, are not accorded the automatic right to decide what is best for others.

Protection from unnecessary pain

Protection from unnecessary pain consists in managing such pain before it occurs. What is 'unnecessary' pain? In this discussion we take it to mean pain that could be prevented or minimized but is not. There are three situations where unnecessary pain ensues.

First, there are some therapeutic activities that result in pain. These include diagnostic techniques such as lumbar puncture, or procedures such as a dressing change. All would agree that such pain occurs; but its short-term nature, the extent to which the desired outcome outweighs the apparently trivial pain, or the desire to get on with the job, have all been used to rationalize the lack of attention paid to the pain incurred. The means exist to minimize the pain, and in many settings pre-procedural analgesics are offered and given. Moreover, sometimes the prevention of unnecessary pain also facilitates treatment. For example, pre-procedural analgesic, given time to be effective, not only minimizes discomfort but allows the procedure to be completed more easily and often more quickly by creating a less anxious and therefore relaxed patient.

Second, there is another source of unnecessary pain that is within the scope of health professionals to manage. The protection of patients from unnecessary pain requires that care is provided by competent practitioners. However, a dilemma can arise between the provision of skilled care and the commitment in many clinical areas to train competent practitioners. In this dilemma, the priority should rest with patient care. Some propose that patients, by choosing a teaching centre for care, implicitly consent to their situation being used as an opportunity for learners to gain necessary experience to become skilled practitioners. Nevertheless, adequate instruction and supervision are essential to protect patients from unnecessary pain caused by inexperienced practitioners, and to this end the United Kingdom Central Council (UKCC) *Code of Professional Conduct* (UKCC, 1984, 1992) prescribes personal responsibility in decisions about who provides care:

> Ensure that no action or omission on his/her part or within his/her sphere of influence is detrimental to the condition or safety of patients/ clients.

A second area of concern where questionable competence could create avoidable discomfort for the patient arises from the lack of recognized preparation, credentials and research-based evidence for many of the non-traditional therapies that are used in pain management. For example, what is the minimum level of knowledge required for competent practice? Does competent and safe practice require supervised clinical experience? When do potentially unsafe clinical circumstances make it inappropriate to suggest the use of the therapy? Patients in pain, particularly those experiencing long-term or severe pain, are drawn by any prospect of relief and so may agree to procedures whose effects are uncertain (Whedon and Ferrell, 1991). At the moment, responsibility for deciding about competency, in the absence of agreed criteria and credentials lies with the individual practitioner—as the UKCC *Code of Professional Conduct* states:

> Acknowledge any limitations of competence and refuse in such cases to accept delegated functions without first having received instruction in regard to those functions and having been assessed as competent.

Third and lastly, unnecessary pain results when knowledge and skills known to be effective in pain management are not used. This leads to the next ethical principle.

Freedom from unwanted pain

A number of reasons have been proposed for the failure to relieve pain (Scott, 1984; McCaffery and Beebe, 1989). The authors believe that in many cases, such failure is avoidable. Certainly, the provision of pain relief requires technical knowledge and skills, but that is not all. It also requires moral commitment, namely to 'ensure the exploration of everything possible within the scope of nursing practice to provide optimum pain relief' (Spross *et al*, 1990). If the means exist to provide adequate pain relief, failure to provide that treatment should be considered unethical professional behaviour.

Nevertheless, in instances when the means are not available to relieve pain, what then is ethical nursing? It is to stay and be present for the person in pain. McCaffery and Beebe (1989) referred to this commitment when they noted that it is important for the nurse to communicate a willingness to 'stay' even when the pain cannot be controlled. 'Staying' means more than being in the same physical space. It is also *being with* the person in pain and breaking through the isolation which was discussed earlier.

Privacy

Finally, pain management raises concern about privacy (Fiser, 1986) and confidentiality, in so far as it involves multiprofessional team work. When a patient discloses intimate details to a particular member of the team, which other members should have access to them? When a multiprofessional team is working well and decision-making is a shared activity, it is sometimes assumed that the patient agrees to the sharing of information. Often they do, but not always.

Where a small and consistent team work together on the premise of shared information, the issue of confidentiality can be explicitly addressed during the admission or initial interview. The patient can be told that their care is planned and carried out by a group of skilled professionals who work together. Information that is shared with one member of the team will be used by the whole team to develop the most effective plan of care. If the patient does not want certain information further disseminated, they have only to say so and the original recipient will keep it in confidence. Thus, the right of the patient to privacy is protected, whilst the need for the communication of relevant information among members of the caring team is made clear.

Pain and death

To die is the most certain event of human life, but the manner of dying is a focal issue of health care. Politicians and lawyers may debate the pros and cons of the law on euthanasia, and philosophers the issues of killing or letting die (Glover, 1977), but day by day nurses and doctors are faced with patients who are dying but wish to live; dying and glad to die; and—most distressingly—living but wishing to die. The existence of pain as a reason for a person's desire to die and the potentially lethal effect of anaesthetic and analgesic drugs focus the dilemmas for doctor, nurse and patient.

The hospice movement has made a major contribution to increasing the quality and quantity of life by the skilful use of drugs and other therapies for pain relief. This progress, however, does not alter the fact that people die, sometimes shortly after receiving an analgesic drug. It is rare for us to know in advance exactly when someone will die, consequently it is possible for nurses, especially novice nurses, to fear or believe that they have unwittingly killed a sick person by administering an analgesic. In discussing the ethical principles of *nonmaleficence* (doing no harm). Beauchamp and Childress (1983) quoted from the Ethical and Religious Directives for Catholic Health as follows:

> It is not euthanasia to give a dying person sedatives and analgesics for the alleviation of pain when such a measure is judged necessary even though they may deprive the patient of the use of reason or shorten his life.

Perhaps one helpful thing nurses can do in grappling with this perennial dilemma is to admit that the problem exists and to acknowledge and discuss the issue with colleagues, patients and their relatives.

Ethical codes

We are not alone in facing ethical dilemmas. All people caring for the sick attempt to decide what is right and wrong in their conduct towards the sick. The British Association of Holistic Health produced a recommended ethical code for its members, not as a substitute for but as an addition to the codes of ethics of practitioners' professional bodies. The following extracts seem particularly helpful in the context of pain nursing (British Holistic Medical Association/British Association of Holistic Health, 1986).

The client:
The practitioner shall recognise the autonomy of the client, acknowledging the client's inner potential and wisdom as well as their pain and suffering.

In recognising the inherent quality and wholeness of each individual, the practitioner shall have respect for all religious, spiritual, political and social views, irrespective of creed, race, sex, colour, political or social ideology.

The practitioner shall at all times respect the confidentiality of the therapeutic relationship and shall not divulge information to anyone, including the client's family, without the client's consent.

The practitioner:
In respect of their own needs, the practitioner shall have recognition for their own limits, physically, emotionally and spiritually. This includes recognising when one's own skills need to be supplemented by others.

The practitioner shall recognise their need for personal, professional and spiritual development. This includes ensuring that they are sufficiently trained and experienced in the therapeutic service(s) they are offering to their clients. It also means being open to further training and development with other therapists.

REFERENCES

Beauchamp TL & Childress JF (1983) *Principles of Biomedical Ethics*, 2nd edn, p 114. Oxford: Oxford University Press.

Benner P (1984) *From Novice to Expert. Excellence and Power in Clinical Nursing Practice*. Menlo Park: Addison-Wesley.

British Holistic Medical Association/British Association of Holistic Health (1986) *Newsletter* 13, pp 16–17. Gloucester Place, London.

Edwards RB (1984) Pain and the ethics of pain management. *Social Science and Medicine* 18 (6): 515–523.

Fiser KB (1986) Privacy and pain. *Philosophical Investigations* 9 (1): 1–17.

Glover J (1977) *Causing Death and Saving Lives*. Harmondsworth: Penguin.

Herth K (1990) Fostering hope in terminally-ill people. *Journal of Advanced Nursing* 15: 1250–1259.

McCaffery M & Beebe A (1989) *Pain: Clinical Manual for Nursing Practice*. St Louis: CV Mosby.

Scott J (1984) *Cancer Pain*. Canada: Department of Health and Welfare.

Spross J, McGuire D & Schmitt R (1990) Oncology Nursing Society Position Paper on cancer pain. *Oncology Nursing Forum* 17: 595–614.

UKCC (1984, 1992) *Code of Professional Conduct for the Nurse, Midwife and Health Visitor*. London: UKCC.

Vaillot M (1970) Hope: The restoration of being. *American Journal of Nursing* 70 (2): 268–273.

Whedon M & Ferrell BR (1991) Professional and ethical considerations in the use of high-tech pain management. *Oncology Nursing Forum* 18 (7): 1135–1143.

6

Pharmacological Management of Pain

Pharmacological interventions have always had a valued place in the history of pain management. The formulation of non-steroidal anti-inflammatory drugs (NSAIDs) and various co-analgesics have expanded the range of available agents beyond opioids. Co-analgesics are drugs that reduce the experience of pain but were primarily or initially used for other effects and were found incidentally to have beneficial effects on pain, or at least on pain with certain types of causes.

Whilst there is much to know about specific agents, the clinical pharmacist and formularies can provide detailed information when required for individual patient management. In this book we concentrate on the process by which drugs are effectively used to manage pain. This process requires the involvement of a variety of people. As McCaffery and Beebe (1989) pointed out, 'the responsibility for pharmacological control of pain rests with the *entire* health-care team'. Each member of the health-care team (primarily the physician and nurse in partnership with the patient) has specialized knowledge that when shared, enhances the effectiveness of any drug regimen that attempts to control pain. This chapter explores the nurse's contribution to this interactive process. Specific areas of nursing involvement to be explored include the following:

1. Influencing prescribing decisions when the regimen is established.
2. Individualizing the regimen.
3. Enhancing the action of the drugs.
4. Preventing or minimizing complications.

5. Monitoring the therapeutic and toxic effects.
6. Ensuring adjustments are made.

In working out these activities, the nurse interacts with both the patient and the physician (Figure 1). Information from each source is integrated, permitting more specific and effective drug regimens to be developed for each individual patient. Some activities primarily seem to reside within the domain of one particular profession, but in actuality, that activity is influenced and shaped by information from the others. Thus whilst the physician prescribes drugs to manage a person's pain, this decision-making is guided not only by medical assessment of the patient along with knowledge of pharmacology, but also by the different assessment information provided by the nurse.

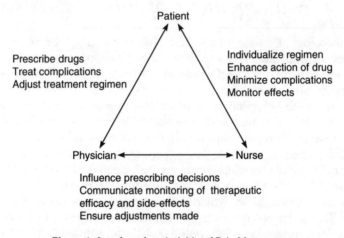

Figure 1. *Interdependent Activities of Pain Management*

INFLUENCING PRESCRIBING DECISION-MAKING

Before examining the particular decisions related to setting up a patient plan, two potential strengths that may underpin the nurse's influence will be mentioned. The first relates to the kind of information that the nurse possesses. This rests on the established relationship and assessment by direct observation of the person in pain. These sources could provide helpful data for the physician to use to prescribe the most effective regimen. For example, how the patient rates the pain needs to be put alongside the functional difficulties the patient experiences because of the pain. Exploring previous painful episodes may indicate that fears of nausea and vomiting or constipation may make a patient reluctant to take a prescribed regimen, suggesting that antiemetics or laxatives should be part of the regimen, rather than added when the side-effect appears.

The second potential strength is the nurses ability to communicate information to the physician and other relevent professionals. Communication skills include being able to identify important facts and present them in a form that is useful for others. Not all the information that the nurse knows about the patient is needed by others, so that selecting and summarizing significant information is vital. With a sound knowledge base and experience, the nurse could become more proficient at recognizing the implications of the information that the assessment has yielded. It may be that the patient has not understood the importance of the details of their experience. The nurse can bring together both that information from the patient, and knowledge about pain, such that the problem is more precisely defined, leading to a more focused approach in the management plan.

Issues of importance to the patient may need to be clearly stated when decisions are being made—for instance, a fear of drowsiness in patients living alone. Sometimes the person in pain can, with encouragement and support, express these concerns. The nurse's skills, in this instance, lies in helping the person 'connect' (Davis and Oberle, 1990) with other important people. At other times the nurse may, with the person's permission, communicate and speak for the patient when decisions are being made and the patient is not present.

Now to turn to the question of what decisions need to be made when establishing a drug plan for a person in pain. Some decisions are related directly to the analgesic and include the choice of a specific drug, the dose, timing and route of administration. The knowledge and beliefs about pain and analgesics that are held by lay and professional people alike will influence this decision.

DRUG ISSUES

Why do nurses need to know about specific drugs—and how much information do they need—since nurses do not prescribe them? It is important to understand why specific agents have been chosen and how they are best administered, for several reasons. In the first place, there is a commitment to provide effective pain relief to people in pain.

Many decisions, even after the drug has been prescribed, are within the nurse's province. Often several drugs are prescribed with a dose range and a 'p.r.n.' (as necessary) status. The choice of drug, dosage and timing may all be decided by the nurse, so it is imperative that the nurse is able to make knowledgeable decisions that will enhance the desired outcome of pain relief. Secondly, patients and families recognize the nurse as a source of information and explanation about why they are taking specific drugs or doing certain activities. This becomes especially important when the person making decisions about when and how much analgesic drug to take is not the professional but the person actually in pain or their family carers, as happens when the person is in their own home. How and what information is presented to the patient partly depends upon their questions and concerns.

Choice of analgesic

Various factors must be taken into account when choosing which drug to prescribe. Three main categories of drugs are used to control pain. These are listed in Table 1. The first point to note is that the different categories of analgesics primarily act by different mechanisms. This means that, especially in severe chronic pain, several avenues of action can be used, while spreading out the side-effects. The same effect (i.e. pain relief) can be potentially achieved using less of each drug while reducing the severity of side-effects produced if a larger dose of either drug were used alone.

The non-opioid drugs have an important role in pain management. At the site of tissue injury, chemicals such as prostaglandins, histamine and bradykinin are released, which cause inflammation and may sensitize the nerve fibres to pain stimulation. Aspirin and the other NSAIDs decrease the inflammatory response and may inhibit the production of prostaglandins both centrally and peripherally (Wall and Jones, 1991). They are often used alone for mild pain but may also be used in combination with opioids for bone pain and other severe pain. In combination with opioids, they may have the effect of allowing less opioids to be used while still relieving pain. Also they produce fewer central nervous system effects, such as sedation or dysphoria. However, the non-opioid analgesics do have side-effects that need to be taken into account: these include increased bleeding time, gastric irritation and allergic responses. In spite of these disadvantages, they are a useful and effective group of drugs. It is unwise to combine them with alcohol.

Opioid drugs are of two different types: agonists (sometimes called

Category	Mechanism	Basic drug	Alternative
Non-opioid drugs	Mainly work in the peripheral tissues, interfering with chemicals (e.g. prostaglandins) that stimulate pain endings	Aspirin (acetylsalicylic acid)	*Over the counter*: paracetamol ibuprofen *Prescription*: indomethacin naproxen Other NSAIDs
Opioid drugs (narcotics)	Mainly work in the brain and spinal cord, inhibiting the transmission of pain	Agonists: codeine morphine Agonist-antagonists: do not use in combination with agonist	Pethidine Dextropropoxyphene Diamorphine Pentazocine Buprenorphine Nalbuphine
Co-analgesic (adjuvant) drugs	Various actions	Nerve compression: corticosteroids Nerve pain: carbamazepine amitriptyline phenytoin Infected fungating lesions: metronidazole Muscle spasms: diazepam Anxiety: diazepam	

Adapted from McCaffery and Beebe (1989) and Scott (1984)

pure agonists) and agonists–antagonists. When drugs of either type are used alone, they relieve pain; when given together, however, the agonist–antagonist binds competitively to the receptors and can even displace already attached agonists at the binding site; these two classes of drugs should therefore not be administered together. Naloxone is a pure antagonist and is used to treat narcotic overdose in the context of life-threatening respiratory depression.

Co-analgesics or adjuvant medications are often used to relieve specific types of pain. Corticosteroids are useful in reducing pains caused by inflammation and swelling, e.g. arthritis, nerve compression and raised intracranial pressure. Tricyclic antidepressants 'have a central analgesic effect on certain types of pain. They are particularly useful in dealing with pain of a neurogenic origin. . . . Such pain may follow nerve damage resulting in deafferentation of a region, or when nerves are partially damaged, resulting in altered sensation' (Diamond and Coniam, 1991). Amitriptyline is an example of this group of drugs. Phenytoin and carbamazepine are anticonvulsants which are effective in controlling intermittent sharp pains such as trigeminal neuralgia.

The intensity of pain is an important factor in the choice of analgesic agent. Pain severity is determined by listening to the patient's report of pain and noting the degree of relief obtained from previous use of drugs. Some drugs manage mild pain, whilst severe pain may require a stronger drug or a combination of differently acting drugs. While there is a wide choice of analgesics available, it may be more useful to become knowledgeable about a few commonly used drugs than to be vaguely acquainted with a long list. Familiarity with aspirin, codeine and morphine are suggested as illustrated in Table 2. Alternatives tend to be used if the person in pain cannot tolerate the first-choice drug.

Dose

The effective analgesic dose varies from person to person. The right dose is one that relieves pain (Twycross, 1984). Familiarity with a specific type of pain may give the doctor or nurse a notion of the possible range of dose, but that is always tentative until tested on a specific patient. The dose is partly determined by the severity of the pain a person is experiencing, so although a dose of analgesic is ordered, its effect is monitored dose by dose at the beginning until an appropriate dose is found.

With non-opioid analgesics, there is a ceiling effect: that is, beyond a certain dosage, increased analgesia will not occur. With opioids, however, such a ceiling of analgesic effect does not seem to exist, the major

Table 2. Basic analgesic choices.

Pain severity	Analgesic choice
Mild	Aspirin Paracetamol Non steroidal anti-inflammatory drug
Mild to moderate	Codeine Aspirin + Codeine Paracetamol + Codeine
Moderate to severe	Codeine Morphine
Severe	Morphine Diamorphine

limitation being the side-effects. As mentioned earlier, when the dilemma arises that severe pain requires a large dose to relieve it adequately but side-effects cause concern, a combination of an opioid and a non-opioid drug can be valuable.

Anticipation of side-effects, particularly respiratory depression and sedation, also influences the dose that is established. There is a range of doses that will effectively produce analgesia while minimizing the experience of sedation. The zone of effectiveness will vary from individual to individual, and it may need an experimental period with the patient to work out the appropriate dose.

Administration

There are other factors besides dosage that will influence the effectiveness of an analgesic regimen, and two major aspects are the nature of the pain and its time scale. Characteristics of analgesic use in acute and chronic pain are compared in Table 3. Some pains (such as postoperative pain) which change rapidly and are expected to be of limited duration need analgesics to be administered in such a way as to allow re-evaluation at regular intervals. Rapid onset of action is also desirable. Chronic pain, which is continuous and changes much more slowly, requires a different schedule of analgesic administration. Analgesics for chronic pain, especially severe pain, should be administered on a regular basis with the aim of maintaining continuous blood levels of the drug—though this will not guarantee that the patient with chronic pain will be pain free. Whichever type of pain patients experience, it is important that they do not worry that they will be left in pain because of indecision, delay or a lack of concern. Anxiety, a major component of unrelieved pain in both acute and chronic pain, is diminished with adequate, continuous pain relief, which in turn leads to the potential for lower doses of analgesic drugs to be required.

Table 3. Comparison of analgesic use in acute and chronic pain.

	Acute	*Chronic*
Aim	Pain relief	Pain relief
Sedation	May be desirable	Usually undesirable
Desired duration of effect	Variable: 2–4 hours to allow for re-evaluation	As long as possible
Timing	As required (on demand)	Regularly (in anticipation)
Dose	Usually standard	Individually determined
Route	Injection or by mouth	By mouth
Co-analgesics	Uncommon	Common

Adapted from Twycross (1984).

In discussing the second issue of timing, duration of action becomes important in situations where the administration of a specific drug is prescribed at longer intervals than the drug is effective. Various drugs not only have a different duration of activity, but if the drug is given intermittently in response to the patient's request instead of regularly, there is a lag between when the patient needs pain relief, when the drug is administered and when it becomes effective. This is pictured in Figure 2.

Various routes of administration and the physiological status of the patient also influence the rapidity with which a drug will begin its action. Decisions about route are motivated by the speed of effect needed and the ease of administration for the patient and carers.

In summary, the choice, dosage, route and frequency of pharmacological intervention need to be appropriate to the age, size and pathology of the person in pain. The ability of the patient's alimentary tract, muscles, circulation, liver, kidneys, lungs and skin to absorb, utilize, metabolize and excrete drugs will crucially affect the relief of pain and side-effects experienced.

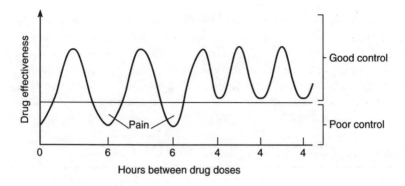

Figure 2. *Effect of timing of drug administration on pain relief.*

INDIVIDUALIZING THE REGIMEN

Effective use of pharmacological agents does not end when a drug regimen has been prescribed. Adaptation may be required to target the regimen more specifically for each particular pain and each unique individual. Individualization has already begun in the prescribing decisions of drug, dose and route of administration. To continue the process requires more information and evaluation.

The process of individualization works through three questions:

1. What is desirable?
2. What is possible?
3. What is acceptable?

First, we should consider who answers these questions. Several people could—the doctor, the nurse, the family and the person in pain. Whilst it would be easy if everyone had the same answer, more often priorities are negotiated to establish the most effective and satisfying plan.

Usually there is agreement on the question of what is desirable. A perfect drug regimen would be characterized by effective analgesia (no pain), no side-effects and no disruption in the person's usual lifestyle. Health-care practitioners often focus on the first two factors and the patient and family add the last one. However, the ideal regimen unfortunately is not always possible. Effective analgesia with a drug regimen is theoretically possible, but limitations are imposed by side-effects that are potentially life-threatening, such as respiratory

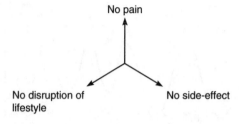

Figure 3. *Aims in individualizing a pain relief regimen.*

depression, or are perceived to be worse than the pain itself, such as drowsiness. So in reality, individualizing is a balancing act (Figure 3).

Sometimes the nature of the pain determines the balance. For intense short-term pain, for example during surgery, sedation and respiratory depression are present but are tolerated and monitored continuously by an anaesthetist. Lifestyle is suspended most dramatically during surgery. In contrast, in chronic pain such as that caused by osteoarthritis, the impact of a drug regimen on lifestyle assumes more importance and a different balance is sought.

Already the questions of acceptability are emerging. The range of possibilities is sifted and weighed by the person in pain, who answers the third question about acceptability. Lifestyle evolves from a unique set of decisions taken by an individual. Therefore, the definition of what balance is acceptable will also be unique. Helping patients articulate and express their priorities and values and finding creative ways to honour these considerations is one of the satisfying aspects of care for many nurses.

Sometimes there is an attempt to work out an administration schedule that supports patient independence. For some patients, minimizing side-effects may be a major focus, whilst for others, attempts to complement and enhance analgesia using non-pharmacological measures are helpful. In all of these attempts, the patient is the final decision-maker—if not in theory, then in practice by rejecting or by accepting and participating in the plan.

ENHANCING ACTION

Since pain is a multidimensional phenomenon with many factors contributing to it, these factors can be modified to achieve the goal of analgesia. For example, the anxiety that often accompanies pain may be addressed, and patient control and involvement may be encouraged and supported.

For some people the experience of pain can create a sense of powerlessness. Such patients require allies and aides to confront the many ways that pain strips their ability to live the way they desire. The frustration of weakness as well as the fear of dependency can magnify the perception and experience of pain. There are many ways that powerlessness may be further underscored: experiencing continuous pain, being dependent on others for drug administration, not knowing why pain is present or for how long it can be expected to last. As these issues are addressed the patient may be delivered out of the power of pain. This deliverance in turn may reduce the level of pain perceived by the individual and the amount of analgesic needed.

Patient-controlled analgesia (PCA) (Ferrante *et al*, 1990) is a strategy for dealing with acute pain. It not only facilitates individualization of drug administration but also supports the patient's contribution to the management of the pain. There was initial reluctance by health-care professionals to promote PCA where strong analgesic drugs such as opioids were used, for fear of potentially life-threatening side-effects and addiction. However, it has been demonstrated that patients can safely administer their own medication and achieve a high quality of analgesia without excessive dosage (Hull, 1985). Administration for postoperative pain is accomplished by first finding the effective analgesic dose for the patient and then giving the patient the power to administer small bolus doses as soon as pain recurs, to maintain analgesia. The prevention of drug overdose is achieved by a timing device, which delays the next dose until the drug already demanded and given has had a chance to work. In the short-term, changing course of postoperative pain, regular and frequent evaluation of the patient's condition is required.

What is important with PCA is the element of control that is exercised by the patient. When patients know they can administer the analgesic as soon as they experience pain, the fear which is part of the power of pain in this situation is confronted. Patients lose the fear that future pain will go unrelieved, as a result of another person's indecision, delay or lack of concern and the reduced anxiety levels help to diminish pain and discomfort. Interestingly, studies of PCA have revealed another aspect of patient control, which is the patient's reluctance to assume responsibility. Bonica (1990) in one study of postoperative pain reported that 85% of patients obtained good to excellent analgesia. However, 15% of the sample had problems: 10% failed to understand the concept of analgesia on demand and how to use the mechanical drug delivery system, and another 5% preferred drug administration by nursing staff to self-administration. Taking control demands information and confidence, and the decision of the patient that they wish to do so. The choice is always the patient's. Research into PCA has been reviewed by Shade (1992).

In chronic pain conditions, the principles are the same. Fear of unrelieved pain intensifies the feelings of powerlessness. In addition to the search for the best balance for the patient of analgesia, side-effects and desired lifestyle, the patient can be helped to gain more control through knowledge about the drugs being used. Information about why and how analgesics work facilitates decisions that will increase the chance of these drugs being effective. For example, patients in chronic pain need to know that regular drug administration results in maintained analgesia and smaller amounts of drug being needed than if the pain is allowed to increase to severe levels. Also, patients need to develop the confidence to make decisions and carry out procedures safely and effectively, otherwise more anxiety is created which would be counterproductive to effective analgesia.

Another strategy to enhance a drug regimen is to combine it with other methods that work in different ways. A variety of techniques are available and are discussed in the following chapter.

PREVENTING OR MANAGING COMPLICATIONS

All medications have desired and undesired effects, and the balancing that is done in establishing an effective regimen has been identified earlier. The issue at hand is how to manage the undesired effects that for some patients can be worse than the pain itself. Nursing involvement may be anticipatory, vigilant or reactive.

To make decisions about the nature of nursing involvement, it helps to know the incidence of a particular side-effect. If a side-effect is certain to occur, anticipatory action is indicated. The nurse prepares the patient for its appearance and, with the doctor; provides a means to manage it. For example, opioids bind to receptors in the gastrointestinal tract causing decreased peristalsis and diminished secretions; this is the underlying mechanism of opioid-induced constipation, and thus constipation is expected to be present in everyone receiving opioids. Therefore, the patient should be told about this side-effect and a concurrent plan established to prevent and or manage it. Stool softeners and peristaltic stimulants will be needed, as well as prophylactic measures such as increased fluids and activity. Regular observation for constipation also needs to be built into evaluation schemes.

Other side-effects of opioids such as nausea and vomiting occur with less frequency and often decrease after a week or two of opioid use. Nausea is induced via several mechanisms. The drug itself may stimulate the vomiting centre in the brain. The effect on the gastrointestinal tract can also result in delayed gastric emptying, producing nausea and vomiting. Anxieties and fears related to pain and the meaning of pain can also contribute to nausea. The nurse could take an anticipatory and preventative approach so that an antiemetic is available and given on a regular basis when the drug regimen is initiated. Another approach could be, 'Be prepared for the worst but hope for the best!' An antiemetic could be available, i.e. ordered by the physician and at hand for p.r.n. administration, and the patient monitored vigilantly during the first couple of doses for the appearance of nausea and vomiting. If the patient did experience these effects they could be treated immediately, minimizing patient distress. Either approach is appropriate and which one is chosen depends on the patient's anxieties, physician preference and nursing style.

Other undesired effects appear infrequently and are unpleasant but not life-threatening. In these cases careful monitoring, knowing the association of the side-effect with the drug, is an appropriate response. Some side-effects are dose-related. The nurse needs to be familiar with the range of potential effects, their incidence and implications.

EVALUATION

Effective pain management requires fine tuning. This fine tuning or titration begins by comparing the desired effect with the actual experience of the patient. The assessment data are used as a baseline to measure the effectiveness of the prescribed regimen and nursing support in achieving pain relief for the patient. Considerations for evaluation include:

1. How much pain is the person experiencing?
2. Does the medication ever take the pain away completely? (Are the drug and the dose adequate for the pain that the patient is experiencing?)
3. Does the pain return before it is time for the next dose of medication? (Is the interval of administration adequate?)

4. What undesired effects does the patient experience?
5. In what activities is the patient able to engage?
6. What is the influence of other pain-relieving measures?

Many care settings will use a flow sheet to record observations about these questions. These need to contain repeated evaluations of pain, pain interventions, other symptoms and activities—indeed whatever is relevant to the progress of the particular person. These sheets show the path of a patient's pain management with drugs in a single document. The information is concise and standardized, and becomes a reliable basis for decisions about drug adjustments.

Evaluation will be frequent, often with every dose, at the initiation of a drug regimen or after changes to it. As the regimen is tailored to the patient and the pain is controlled, regular but less frequent evaluations are made. Patients can and should be involved in this process by doing the assessment and recording the details on the chart, if they desire. Active patient involvement provides direct information from the patient about the pain. It also assists in communication between patients and health-care professionals by giving the patient a guide to the type of information that doctors and nurses need in order to evaluate pain and make decisions about changes to the drug plan. Also, patients are able to understand that health-care professionals have a continuing interest in their pain problem. Finally, this involvement supports the patients' sense of control by giving them a legitimate and valuable role in their own care.

Whilst patient participation may appear to require less nursing time (due to the patient filling in the sheet), in fact there is a necessity for different nursing support, such as giving information about the rationale for the various types of drugs, and instructions on how to reliably evaluate and fill in the various documents. The nurse still will have to use the information that the patient has gathered to continue the 'fine tuning'.

ADJUSTMENT OF THE REGIMEN IF REQUIRED

Pain relief that is acceptable to the patient is the desired goal. This may be accomplished with feedback to and discussion with the prescribing physician, and adjustment to the regimen made and evaluated. The doctor needs concise, accurate and reliable information about the pain, the regimen and the patient's response. The pain flow sheet is important as a tool to help provide this information.

At times the pain may be difficult to manage and a commitment to continue to work toward the goal of acceptable pain relief is important. Patients need to know that their pain is an important issue for their carers and that they will not be abandoned to suffer. Specialized expertise may be needed if the knowledge and skills of the existing team cannot adequately address the pain.

In summary, the nurse's role in using pharmacological agents for pain relief is challenging. The interaction between the person in pain, the nurse and the doctor continues through all the phases discussed. Because each patient is unique, the process will develop differently each time, and the challenge to the nurse is to use flexible and creative assessment skills, clinical judgement and communication skills in such a way that the contribution of drugs to the management of pain is maximized for the patient's benefit.

REFERENCES

Bonica JJ (ed.) (1990) *The Management of Pain*, 2nd edn. Philadelphia: Lea & Febiger.

Davis B & Oberle K (1990) Dimensions of the supportive role of the nurse in palliative care. *Oncology Nursing Forum* 7 (1): 87–94.

Diamond AW & Conium SW (1991) *The Management of Chronic Pain*, p 64. Oxford: Oxford University Press.

Ferrante FM, Ostheimer GW & Covino BG (eds) (1990) *Patient Controlled Analgesia*, 2nd edn. Oxford: Blackwell Scientific.

Hull CJ (1985) Opioid infusions for the management of post-operative pain. In Smith G & Covino BG (eds) *Acute Pain*. London: Butterworth.

McCaffery M & Beebe A (1989) *Pain: Clinical Manual for Nursing Practice*, p 42. St Louis: CV Mosby.

Scott J (1984) *Cancer Pain*. Ottawa: Ministry of Health and Welfare.

Shade P (1992) Patient-controlled analgesia: can client education improve outcomes? *Journal of Advanced Nursing* 17: 408–413.

Twycross RG (1984) Relief of pain. In Saunders C (ed.) *The Management of Terminal Malignant Disease*, 2nd edn, pp 64–90. London: Edward Arnold.

Wall PD & Jones M (1991) *Defeating Pain. The War Against a Silent Epidemic*. London: Plenum Press.

7

Non-pharmacological Management of Pain

Whilst the use of drugs constitutes a major and effective strategy for pain relief, it is not by any means the only strategy. The experience of pain can be modified by the use of non-pharmacological methods, some of which traditionally fall within the nurse's scope of practice. These include physical techniques such as the use of heat and cold and massage, as well as psychological or cognitive interventions such as distraction and imagery. Usually the effects are temporary, but occasionally long-lasting reduction in pain results. The 'gate' in the spinal cord may be closed via afferent peripheral and/or descending central effects, and patterns of nerve firing may be modified in some chronic pain states.

Non-pharmacological interventions may be used alone as a primary management strategy in mild and brief pains. In moderate or severe pain, these techniques may have a synergistic effect when added to the drug regimen but are unlikely to eliminate the pain on their own, and are usually complementary to rather than an alternative to drug regimens. The use of many strategies to help people with intractable pain was summarized by Wall (1984):

> Combination, alteration and circulation of therapies may well be the best tactic to defeat the homeostatic abilities of nervous mechanisms to restore pathological states.

In a study of 190 elderly people with persistent or recurrent pain living in the community (Walker *et al*, 1990), it was found that the majority of people took analgesics, and many also used non-pharmacological strategies including exercise, heat, topical applications, dressings, massage and physiotherapy.

Patients may want to use one or several of these techniques to add non-pharmacological elements to their pain management regimen. In chronic pain, when the patient has to adapt to pain that may not be eliminated completely, these techniques are especially important. As discussed in Chapter 6, the aim is to balance the benefits of drug-produced analgesia with the side-effects of those drugs that affect physical and psychological functioning. The strategies discussed in this chapter may offer therapeutic techniques that synergistically enhance the drug effectiveness, they may promote the use of a smaller dose to achieve the same analgesic effect, or they may be used as the sole intervention.

Patients and family members may find that these techniques provide an opportunity for their active involvement in the management of the pain, thus furnishing them with a practical way to deal with feelings of helplessness or forced dependency on others. Because some of these strategies are self-initiated and can be carried out independently, particularly relaxation, distraction or imagery, this shift in initiation and performance from others to self fosters a sense of power and control. Also, these techniques can be performed at a convenient time for the patient. Self-management decreases the constraints imposed by relying on another's knowledge, skills and time. Many patients worry about imposing on other people's willingness to be involved, and to stay involved. Finally, we know that pain can create difficulties in family relationships. When the patient is able to perform these techniques independently, the family may to some extent be able to maintain the demarcation between their role as family members and the role of family as carer.

These techniques have an exciting potential (for both patient and nurse) to deal with pain in an increasingly effective manner. However, it is essential that issues of safety and effectiveness are critically evaluated so that the patient is protected from either unnecessary physical harm or disappointment as a result of unfulfilled claims (Whedon and Ferrell, 1991). These techniques are still the subject of research, and consequently confidence in their use may not be shared by members of the health-care team. A major consequence of operating from an evolving knowledge base is that issues of safety become prominent, and an attitude of caution and vigilance needs to be adopted. Without the confidence given by research-based knowledge, the nurse has several responses. Before offering these techniques, the nurse must prepare to practise safely, that is to anticipate side-effects and monitor for unanticipated ones. Since data are sparse about the use of these methods in specific clinical situations, the nurse will need to integrate what is known about the patient's physiological condition with knowledge about the known effects of the suggested technique. Secondly, while it is important that these techniques are offered in a positive manner, uncritical enthusiasm not only is unwarranted but can in fact create unrealistic expectations by the patient, and lead to the erosion of trust in the nurse as a knowledgeable practitioner, if those expectations are not met. Lastly, caution does not mean non-use. It is precisely this kind of knowledge, which is embedded in clinical practice, that needs to be articulated and tested in a research context, i.e. systematically and rigorously. Well-controlled research in this area is scarce, and double-blind trials impossible. Therefore, to begin the process, the details of how the technique was used and the patient's responses should be meticulously described. The nurse practitioner using these clinical observations combined with specialized research knowledge and skills can begin to provide the research-based knowledge that is needed.

Some of these techniques seem terribly ordinary. Activities of ordinary life that are taken for granted may lead to their value being overlooked. Some of these strategies may already be part of the patient's repertoire to deal with pain (Barbour *et al*, 1986). The nurse builds on that existing foundation. In using these 'ordinary' strategies in a therapeutic setting, the partnership with the patient, which is so important in this area of care, is underscored. For the nurse, these strategies constitute traditional nursing comfort measures and may therefore be forgotten or undervalued as a therapeutic activity. They can be effective and should be used deliberately.

It may take several occasions of use to judge if a particular method is effective, so repeat the trial several times. Using an adequate trial is important when working with carers who need to understand the rationale, objectives, limitations and the need to persist long enough to give the method a fair trial.

The response may be manifested as a change in the character of the pain rather than in diminished intensity, which whilst not eliminating the pain may render the pain more acceptable to the patient. Alternatively the pain may be unchanged, but the patient may be less anxious, less depressed, more active or more able to cope.

These methods are simple, inexpensive and for the most part have minimal complications. Personal preference, experience and patient response will guide choice. Concerns about safety which provide boundaries and contraindications are discussed for each specific strategy.

PHYSICAL INTERVENTIONS

Massage

Massage is the manipulation of soft body tissue by hand for therapeutic purposes. It is a technique that is readily available at home as well as in the hospital. Patient effort and involvement is minimal, which can be important when the patient's energy or function is limited. It also affords carers who otherwise may feel helpless, an opportunity to contribute to the patient's care.

How does massage alter the pain experience? The gate control theory offers one suggestion; the large diameter A-beta fibres which are activated by skin stimulation may close the gate and prevent pain impulses from continuing on to the central nervous system, or alter their character such that the pain is experienced in a different but acceptable way. Massage also increases blood flow to the area, creating a sense of warmth and relaxation. It may also be a form of distraction, temporarily capturing attention and thus altering the perception of pain. Finally, it has been suggested that some types of skin stimulation may promote the release of endorphins, the body's natural morphine (McCaffery and Beebe, 1989).

Massage may involve different strokes which are used for different purposes. Usually the site chosen for massage is that directly over or around the pain. If this is not possible, for example because of broken skin, swelling, fracture or bruising, then the area chosen can be proximal to the pain ('between pain and brain') or contralateral to the painful site, i.e. at a similar site on the opposite side of the body.

Finally, massage as a form of touch is more than just a technical procedure. It is a form of communication that transmits a powerful message of connectedness and acceptability. However, as a culturally interpreted sign of intimacy, touch in massage may require that the nurse be particularly sensitive when exploring this technique. Instead of back and body rubs, massage of feet and hands may be more acceptable.

Physiotherapists who are skilled in this technique will also be a resource when learning about massage.

Local heat

The use of heat has for centuries been a healing and pain-relieving activity and thermal waters and warm sand featured at popular spas down through the ages. It is a measure frequently used by patients for pain when they are in their own setting, such as the application of a hot-water bottle for muscle cramping or low back pain. In a survey among cancer patients to identify non-pharmacological methods of pain relief and their effectiveness, heat methods were used most frequently and helped control pain to some degree in 68% of patients (Barbour *et al*, 1986).

The use of external heat to a local area of the body results in several effects that may begin to explain the impact on pain. First, large fibres may be stimulated and may inhibit or alter the transmission of painful input from the small fibres at the level of the gate system in the spinal cord. Second, vasodilation may increase blood supply to the local area, and this may account for the reduction in pain, particularly if the pain is due to ischaemia. Third, heat can enhance the resolution of a super-ficial local inflammatory response which may have created pain by the swelling that often characterizes an inflammation, such as superficial boils. Fourth, heat may enhance relaxation in muscles, thus relieving the muscle spasm of strenuous exercise or menstrual cramping. Peri-stalsis may be reduced and gastric acid production inhibited by the application of heat for 5–10 minutes to the abdomen, which may be useful in a context of colic. Finally, whilst these are all local effects and as such limited to the specific area of application, many people feel a generalized relaxation when heat is applied, which may reduce their experience of pain.

The methods for applying heat are convenient, and often use water to enhance the conduction and intensity of both heat and cold. The body part may be immersed in warm water, such as in a sitz-bath (a bath in which one sits), or for example soaking an ankle 24 hours after a sprain injury. Asking arthritic patients to save their washing-up until the morning is a practical way to encourage the immersion in warm water of stiff and painful hands (often a feature of early morn-ings). Alternatively, the heat source may be a heating pad or hot-water bottle, or a cloth that has been warmed in hot water or in a microwave oven. With each of these, special care must be taken to prevent scal-ding and thermal damage. Finally, wrapping the body part together with the heat source will help to maintain the heat for longer. In the application of local heat, materials that are commonly available and inexpensive are used. Each of these applied moist heat (or cold) sour-ces must be sealed to prevent leaking, flexible to follow body contours and comfortable for the patient.

There are three cautions that need to be mentioned in the use of heat. First, if there is an active disease process still taking place that would be exaggerated by heat, then heat should not be used. For example, if bleeding is actually or possibly occurring, the application of heat and the resultant vasodilation may result in increased bleeding. The same principle operates with oedema that is evolving immediately following trauma. A wise rule of thumb is to use cold for the first 24 hours following the injury, and then to use heat or cold.

Second, heat should be applied at a comfortable level for the patient. Skin and tissue thermal damage may be caused by prolonged or intense heat. This risk is especially important when the patient either has an altered ability to perceive heat, for instance in scar tissue or areas of anaesthesia, or when the patient has difficulty communicating, such as when there are language difficulties or the patient is unconscious. In these cases, it may be prudent not to use heat.

Finally, when a large area of the body is heated, if the patient stands upright quickly, there is the possibility of orthostatic hypotension due to vasodilation.

Local cold

Cold is not only an effective non-pharmacological method of pain management, it is often more effective than heat (LaFoy and Geden, 1989). However, it is not used as frequently as heat, and does not have the same connotation of relaxation or comfort. A lack of familiarity can result in a reluctance to try cold. In one study where cold sitz-baths were being evaluated for postpartum perineal pain, 119 women refused to participate in the study because they did not want to use the cold immersion for their pain. Even more extreme were the 58 women who said they would not take a cold sitz-bath no matter how severe their pain (Ramler and Roberts, 1986). In another study, patients with rheumatoid arthritis and knee pain had a heating or cooling device placed around one knee. Patients preferred heat, in spite of the fact that cooling produced more pain relief (Editorial, 1982).

It is suggested that cold not only 'closes the gate' by stimulating the large fibres but also reduces muscle spasm by influencing the biochemical activity within muscles (Lehmann, 1982). Cold produces vasoconstriction which in turn may decrease the inflammatory response and oedema production in tissue damage. In acute trauma, cold may reduce histamine release which is thought to enhance the sensitivity of nerve endings to painful stimuli. Cold also increases gastrointestinal peristalsis as well as gastric acid production. It has been found that the analgesic effect of cold lasts longer than the effect of heat owing to the vasoconstriction, which slows the resolution to normal temperature.

Cold is especially useful for pain relief in the first 12–24 hours following acute but not severe trauma, such as some sport injuries. In rheumatoid arthritis during an active inflammatory phase, cold can not only offer pain relief but may also deactivate destructive joint enzymes (McCaffery and Beebe, 1989). In pain caused by vasodilation, as in vascular headaches, it is especially helpful.

The application of cold is convenient and practical, using commonly available materials. As with heat, immersion of the painful part or local application is used. Rubbing the skin with ice for 10 minutes produces local anaesthesia and can be used as a pre-procedural, short-term superficial anaesthetic. Because direct contact with a cold source can be uncomfortable, often the skin is protected by using layers of cloth between the cold source and the skin. When water is added to ice, a constant low temperature is achieved.

The use of cold should not be painful or uncomfortable for the patient. Caution is needed when the patient has decreased or absent communication skills, since patient comfort is a major safety boundary in the use of cold. In clinical conditions where there is impaired circulation, such as in arterial insufficiency or peripheral vascular disease, the use of cold is contraindicated. Since it can provoke increased gastric acidity, it should not be used in the presence of a peptic ulcer.

Table 1 compares the use of massage, heat and cold in pain relief.

Other cutaneous therapies

Other cutaneous interventions used to relieve pain require specialist training (Table 2), for example *transcutaneous electrical nerve stimulation* (TENS), the transmission of electrical energy across the surface of the skin to the nervous system (Mannheimer, 1985; Thompson, 1986; Latham, 1987, 1991; McCaffery and Beebe, 1989); *acupressure*, the application of pressure to acupuncture sites (in Japan called *shiatsu*); and skin-invasive *acupuncture*, the ancient Chinese use of needling of skin points related to meridians or channels through which the life force (*ch'i*) flows (Duffin, 1985; Richardson and Vincent, 1986). These therapies have the ability to produce localized analgesia. Acupuncture can produce profound analgesia, such that surgery can be performed without general anaesthesia. This effect is due, at least in part, to the high levels of endorphins that result (Han, 1989).

TENS can be used by patients in their own home once they have learned to use the apparatus. As more patients are using TENS, nurses are increasingly likely to be indirectly or directly involved. Without

Table 1. Comparison of methods of cutaneous stimulation.

	Massage	Heat	Cold
Use	Mild pain Non-localized pain Musculoskeletal pain Soothing and relaxing	Well-localized pain Ischaemic pain Relaxing	Well-localized pain Vascular headaches Rheumatoid arthritis Muscle cramps Ice massage: pre-procedure local anaesthesia
Ease of administration	Time-consuming Patient effort minimal, but requires another person	Preparation time	Preparation time
Safety concerns	Contraindications: increased bleeding time injured/broken skin thrombophlebitis lymphoedema metastatic bone disease	Burns to skin Caution if active evolving inflammatory or bleeding process	Patient comfort Wrap to avoid direct contact
Cost	Oil, lotion or powder to ease friction	Minimal equipment, commonly available	Minimal equipment, commonly available
Other comments	Issues of modesty because of touch and disrobing (massage feet and hands instead) Increased circulation in local area Not for use on open lesions	Common experience Vasodilation Decreased peristalsis Orthostatic hypotension	Vasoconstriction Increased peristalsis

Table 2. Some specialist therapies for pain management.

Cutaneous therapies
Transcutaneous electrical nerve stimulation
Acupressure
Acupuncture

Behaviour therapies
Hypnosis
Biofeedback
Operant conditioning
Modelling techniques

Psychotherapeutic counselling

---

special training they should not be wholly responsible. The apparatus consists of a power source (with batteries), the electrical output of which is controlled by the setting of dials; two or more leads; and flexible skin electrodes—rather like a personal stereo with electrodes in place of ear phones. The siting of the electrodes, the amplitude of the current and the length of time for which TENS is used are pragmatic decisions dependent on what reduces or eliminates the person's pain. As the effect is localized the electrodes are generally placed over or near to the site of pain, e.g. on either side of an incisional wound for postoperative pain, or over the painful part of an aching back or limb. Skin irritation occurs in some instances and electrodes should never be placed on damaged skin. TENS should not be used by people with pacemakers, nor over sites of the body in which the electrical current could interfere with cardiac rhythms (e.g. carotid sinuses, heart or pregnant uterus). It is inadvisable for people who have 'fits' to use TENS on the head or neck. TENS reduces or eliminates some people's pain only while it is being used, but has a longer-lasting effect for others. We cannot yet predict who will feel most benefit.

COGNITIVE INTERVENTIONS

Cognitive strategies are those in which deliberate effort is devoted to thinking in ways that may minimize the perception and experience of pain. They include distraction, imagery, fantasy and self-statements (positive thoughts of oneself). These interventions range from the everyday distractions which divert attention from pain, to sophisticated meditative states (Worthington, 1978; Fernandez, 1986).

A number of explanations have been put forward as to why particular strategies work. As the pain experience includes sensory, emotional and cognitive aspects, alterations in any or all of these aspects can be beneficial. Some researchers into the use of cognitive techniques have hypothesized that different strategies may influence one dimension of pain (sensory, emotional/motivational and evaluative) more than another. Hackett and Horan (1980) reported a laboratory study of pain induced by the cold-pressor technique in which immersion of a limb in circulating ice water (maintained at 2°C or lower produces a continuous aching or crushing pain) in 81 women; the subjects used relaxation as a strategy to cope with the sensory/ discriminative dimension, distraction (mental arithmetic, imagery) to cope with the emotional dimension and self-instructed coping statements to deal with cognitive/evaluative dimensions. It was concluded that relaxation training increased tolerance to pain, distraction and imagery produced a higher pain threshold, but the self-statements did not have any positive outcome. It is tempting but probably naive to assume that identical outcomes would occur outside the laboratory for people with pain, but at least such research does support the contention that cognition can alter the pain experience. The research findings of Rosensteil and Keefe (1983) demonstrated that coping strategies effective in experimentally induced pain are *not* effective in chronic pain.

The complexity of the relationship between pain experiences and psychological status was illustrated by another laboratory cold-pressor study. The researchers posed the question, 'Can anxiety help us tolerate pain?' (Mustafa and Rokke, 1991). Subjects who were given anxiety-provoking information about the actual pain which was inflicted, experienced more pain than subjects who were given anxiety-provoking information about an irrelevant potential shock (which they did not receive). The researchers concluded that if the person is not anxious it would be unhelpful to make them so, even about irrelevant events; but if a person *is* anxious, e.g. about surgery or unexplained pain, 'rather than reducing anxiety, an alternative approach to treatment might be to help that individual redirect the focus of his or her concerns by making alternative attribution for their arousal' (Mustafa and Rokke, 1991).

Studies of the coping strategies of people who have existing pain confirm that what people believe and how they think does affect their pain experience. For example, Keefe *et al* (1991) analysed the pain and pain coping strategies of people who had knee replacements for rheumatoid arthritis. They found that patients who rated their ability to control and decrease their pain 'high', and who rarely engaged in catastrophizing (imagining the worst), had much lower levels of pain and psychological disability than other patients who did not feel 'in control'. It also seems that what people believe will determine their willingness to use cognitive coping strategies. In a study of pain beliefs and the use of cognitive coping strategies, Williams and Keefe (1991) found that patients who believed that their pain was enduring and mysterious were less likely to use cognitive coping strategies (e.g. reinterpretation of pain sensations), more likely to catastrophize and less likely to rate their coping strategies as effective in controlling and decreasing pain than patients who believed their pain to be understandable and of short duration.

It is important to find a strategy or strategies which work for the individual. Chapman (1984) suggested that because a person uses a particular strategy, it does not follow that it is necessarily the most effective. Suggestions may come from anyone—nurse, the person in pain, family or other carers—but it is only the person in pain who can know what is acceptable, plausible and effective.

We can hypothesize that these cognitive effects are mediated via descending inhibitory pathways in the central nervous system on the gate control mechanism, and/or there are alterations in levels of endorphins and other neurochemicals and in the endocrine or immune systems. Mostly we do not know exactly what is happening in the anatomy and physiology of the person in pain. Some patients may be helped to believe in and understand cognitive interventions by biological explanations, others by psychological theories.

Psychological explanations include the following. Distraction alters the focus of attention. Relaxation, by reducing anxiety and tension levels, can break the pain–tension–anxiety cycle. Patient control by such methods may increase the self-appraisal of power which is a major determinant of emotional state (Russell, 1978). This control is considered an important determinant of pain, especially chronic pain, which otherwise can result in helplessness and despair. Fernandez (1986) suggested that as psychological variables influence pain, including anxiety, predictability, perceived controllability, attention (and others), cognitive strategies that influence these variables constitute a major approach to the management of pain.

Distraction

Distraction has been mentioned throughout this book, including the care studies on pages 145–152. As distraction is an everyday experience it is easy to take it for granted, but the deliberate choice of distraction as a strategy to reduce pain experiences may require some planning for success. As stated earlier, distraction removes pain from the focus of attention at least for a while, so that pain tolerance is increased. It probably has no lasting effect on the pain, but can give temporary relief from continuing acute and chronic pains and may render a brief nociceptive pain (e.g. an injection) less noticeable. Distraction may, in part, explain the phenomenon of 'injury without pain', though most casual distractions and nurse–patient interactions have less profound effects on pain.

Psychological explanations of distraction are based upon theories about the limited capacity of focal attention (Mackworth, 1976). Although we can do many things at the same time, such as control bodily functions, perform skilled activities (drive a car, play the piano) and talk or sing simultaneously, in normal states of consciousness we are focally aware of only one (or at least a limited aspect of) thought and experience. In addition, our span of concentration has limits, and from time to time we seem to monitor (become focally aware of) ourselves and our environment. At such a time pain could re-emerge into consciousness.

It is crucial that the attention of the person in pain is directed away from pain. Tacit or explicit agreement from the patient is essential for distraction to work. We can turn cartwheels or pull funny faces, but if the thinking of the person with pain is not captured they will not be distracted. The distraction chosen must be interesting to the person in pain—overwhelmingly interesting if possible. Children may be eager and able to name and describe all the monsters they know of; teenagers their favourite sporting heroes, games or songs. Music, books, radio, television, food, conversation—in fact any sensory stimulus may distract.

There are a number of important provisos about the use of distraction. The first has been mentioned earlier in the book: if distraction reduces pain, it does not mean either that the pain was unreal or imaginary, or that the person was exaggerating. There are some pains that seem to preclude the desire or ability to concentrate on thinking of other things—these include migraine. Avoiding fear-provoking stimuli and any that are personally upsetting is obviously desirable but not always predictable. The sensory modality should be appropriate to the person's ability and to the situation in which pain is experienced. For instance, some 'stroke' aphasic people can sing fluently, although unable to converse; however, many investigations require stillness and cooperation with medical instructions, so that singing would be incompatible with, say, successful chest aspiration.

As distraction requires effort it may leave the person tired and even more conscious of any persistent pain. It is a strategy ideally suited to aid a person to cope with potentially painful medical investigations and nursing procedures—not as a substitute for local or regional anaesthesia, but in addition. It is also a strategy that may be helpful during the time it takes for an administered analgesic to become effective. In both these situations, when the investigation is completed or the drug has acted, the person will be pain-free or at least have reduced pain, and be able to relax or sleep after the period of distraction. McCaffery and Beebe discuss distraction techniques and imagery in chapters 6 and 8 of their book, *Pain* (McCaffery and Beebe, 1989).

Imagery

Whereas distraction may arise from personal involvement with external stimuli via any of the senses—touch, sight, hearing, smell or taste—or from internal thoughts, imagery is solely a phenomenon of thinking. Therapeutic imagery is thinking the best—the opposite of catastrophizing (thinking the worst). Images can be roughly divided into three classes:

1.   Images of ourselves.
2.   Images of the outside world.
3.   Images of ourselves in the world.

Whether or not imagery has any fundamental effect on the cause or apparent lack of cause of a pain is debatable, but imagery can certainly add to or reduce fear and tension, and so alter the state of muscle tension and autonomic nervous system activity. People experiencing pain are highly likely to have images of their bodies, especially of the parts of the body that hurt. In an effort to make sense of pains, particularly when the cause is not visible or obvious, they may visualize anatomical changes, e.g. tears, lumps, bleeding, spasms, or non-anatomical analogies of whatever makes sense to them; for example, a pulsating headache may evoke the image of the 'seven dwarfs' hammering on the skull. The way in which patients describe their pain may reveal their imagery.

Nurses have many opportunities to learn about the imagery of patients and to influence its content for better or worse. For instance, what is said about the action of an analgesic or other drug when it is administered can change the image of the pain and of the self, such that the recipient may feel better even before the pharmacological action has had time to occur. Positive imagery may, at least in part, account for the placebo effect of all therapies (a placebo is a vehicle for cure by suggestion and is surprisingly successful, if only temporarily) (Lawrence and Bennett, 1980).

In addition to the introduction of positive ideas (where justified) into conversations with patients, which may influence imagery, planned imagery can be discussed and offered as a pain-relieving strategy. Where time is available and the pain is continuous, imagery is likely to be most effective if the person is comfortable and the environment quiet. In such circumstances *guided imagery* may be useful. Stories or descriptions of journeys may be related by the nurse or other carer, listened to on a tape recording or recalled privately by the person in pain. No overt response is required from the patient, who does not have to speak or act, only listen and follow the thread of the images that are evoked. Such imagery aims to distract and relax.

An alternative type of guided imagery focuses on the source of the pain and attempts to visualize some form of healing process or outcome. To continue the 'thumping headache' theme: Snow White might come along and take the seven dwarfs, with their hammers, home to dinner and so out of the patient's head. Imagery can be fun and include humour. Reflection upon the powerful religious imagery of pain enables some people to cope with and make sense of their own experience. Prayer may evoke positive images. In Friedman's book on chronic pain (Friedman, 1992), she quotes the following passage from *Medical Nemesis* by Illich:

> By transforming pain, illness and death from a personal challenge into a technical problem, medical practice expropriates the potential of people to deal with their human condition in an autonomous way and becomes the source of a new kind of un-health.

Harnessing people's imagery may be a way of returning to the pain patient a resource that was more fully utilized in the pre-mechanistic, pre-Cartesian era.

In summary, distinctions exist between cognition as distraction, in which the focus of attention is captured at least for a while by something other than pain; guided imagery that is used to produce feelings of tranquillity and relaxation (e.g. mental images of walking in a favourite garden or by the seaside); and guided imagery that intentionally focuses on the pain and attempts to reinterpret the sensation or experience (e.g. burning felt as warmth) or reduce the pathology (e.g. by trying to send an army of white cells to shrink a tumour or reduce inflammation). It is, however, unwise to assume that imagery will work as intended, or that all people will be helped by the same images. Professor Hayward (1991) described a person who was told to imagine the pain as an elephant sitting on the chest which, if starved, would gradually reduce in weight and so the pain would fade away. This strategy ceased to be successful after a few days when the patient became concerned for the hungry elephant! As follower of the imagery of 'gliding down a peaceful river' one of the authors chose to imagine a real river and had to stop the imagery abruptly on reaching the weir for fear of shooting over the brink!

The nurse's role in the use of cognitive strategies may be as teacher, assistant or facilitator. Sometimes nurses can assist the person in using mental focusing and distraction strategies, for example by talking, helping to do mental arithmetic, and providing guided imagery ideas or tape recordings for the patient to listen to. Impromptu creativity may be required for distraction from acute, short-lived pains such as occur with invasive investigations or pain-provoking nursing procedures. Active cooperation and creativity are required from the person in pain, whose own thinking (cognition) has to be harnessed if pain perception is to be reduced.

The beauty of cognitive strategies is that they can be learned and used by the pain sufferer. Indeed, we should remember that more and more people are skilled in the use of techniques such as transcendental meditation, yoga and self-hypnosis. Such people may merely need privacy and peace to practise what they already know.

OTHER PSYCHOLOGICAL THERAPIES

Behaviour therapies

Behaviour therapy (see Table 2) includes hypnosis, biofeedback, operant conditioning and modelling techniques (Turk and Flor, 1984). They are usually offered by specialist practitioners, notably psychologists, but are also learned and used by some nurses. With people who have recurrent or persistent pain, these therapies are mostly used in conjunction with physical and pharmacological techniques as part of an overall plan of care.

Hypnosis (Hildegard, 1975; Orme and Dinges, 1984) is an artificially induced passive state in which there is increased amenability and responsiveness to suggestions and commands, provided that these do not conflict seriously with the subject's own conscious or unconscious wishes (definition from *Dorland's Medical Dictionary*). Hildegard (1975) stated that it can be used to suggest pain reduction, alteration in the pain experience and diversion of attention from pain. Distraction, imagery and self-statement have similar aims.

Biofeedback (Flor *et al*, 1983) is primarily an extension of relaxation in which the person learns to gain a measure of control over normally unconscious functions, such as reducing muscle tension or increasing alpha brain activity. Visual feedback of physiological parameters is provided by an electronic monitoring machine (e.g. an electromyograph or electroencephalograph).

Operant conditioning (Fordyce, 1973; Turner and Chapman, 1982) is the rewarding of desired behaviours and the ignoring of undesired behaviours. It is thought that the maladaptive behaviours of some chronic pain sufferers arise and persist because the reward of attention and sympathy has been elicited by pain and incapacity, whereas 'well behaviour' has been punished by expressions of disbelief from friends, family and carers, e.g. 'Your pain can't be too bad or you wouldn't be walking, working, cooking, laughing, etc.'. The aim of operant conditioning is to reverse these experiences so that well behaviour is rewarded and sickness behaviour not rewarded. The outcome if successful is an increase in activity level and a reduced reliance upon medication. The pain *per se* may or may not be reduced.

Modelling techniques encourage the person in pain to copy the behaviour of others. According to Park and Fulton (1991), this technique has been used for acute short-lived pain in children, e.g. videos showing other children's appropriate responses to painful or unpleasant procedures. It is probable that a great deal of modelling occurs as people in pain watch, listen and talk to one another.

It is crucial that the decision to use any of these behavioural interventions is made in the context of a knowledgeable and supportive team of carers, such as may exist in pain clinics. The person in pain must wish to participate, and the nature and causation of their pain must have been fully investigated, otherwise the person may suffer more harm than good. For example rewarding increased activity would be inappropriate if it thereby caused further damage to the body. Withdrawing sympathy from someone with pain could amount to mental cruelty. It is arguably no use achieving therapy goals at the risk of damaging the personality of the pain sufferer. The use of behaviour therapies carries the risk of treating people as something less than fully human (M.F.'s personal prejudice), but in conjunction with other interventions—notably pharmacological and psychotherapeutic support—operant conditioning can play an important part in reducing the negative psychosocial consequences of chronic pain, and all methods may reduce the experience of pain.

Psychotherapeutic counselling

A basic concept of psychotherapeutic counselling is of 'healing through meeting' (Buber, 1966)—not the giving of advice, as the word 'counsel' suggests. The views expressed by two therapists seem particularly helpful in reinforcing the central theme of this book—of being alongside the person in pain, trying to understand pain from their point of view and being willing to learn and change ourselves in the process of interaction. Firstly, psychoanalyst Patrick Casement, in his book *On Learning from the Patient* (Casement, 1985), expresses the danger of seeing what we expect to see instead of the reality for the patient:

> By listening too readily to accepted theories, and to what they lead the practitioner to expect, it is easy to become deaf to the unexpected. When a therapist thinks that he can see signs of what is familiar to him, he can become blind to what is different and strange.

Secondly, Friedman, a pain therapist who uses biofeedback as part of her caring, believes that a 'healing through meeting' perspective between patient and therapist is the fundamental element in the journey toward the alleviation of pain (Friedman, 1992):

> When the patient and the therapist enter into a healing partnership the patient has the opportunity to communicate the underlying aspects of his or her pain.

Patients whose pain is experienced in the context of dramatic and devastating circumstances, requiring major lifestyle adaptations—as a result, for example, of multiple injury, paralysis, amputation, coronary occlusion or terminal illness—are likely to be particularly helped by carers including nurses who are skilled in psychotherapeutic counselling. Both the experience of physical pain and the suffering associated with the loss of the former self can be helped by someone who understands the languages of body, mind and person (Degenaar, 1979). See Table 1 on page 7.

EXERCISE

Exercise is an important strategy in the fight against chronic pain. People can become physically unfit (deconditioned) as a result of enforced immobility, as may occur following injury, surgery or illness. Provided that any accompanying acute pain subsides, such people generally regain their previous level of fitness as they resume their normal lifestyle—even though this may take a surprisingly long time (Fordham, 1985). People who have chronic pain, however, may find that movements and previously enjoyed activities are abandoned in an effort to prevent exacerbation of pain. This is a natural protective response which prevents further injury; stillness is a strategy that aids healing. The dilemma for those who have chronic pain is whether to take the decision that *activity despite pain* is worth risking. There are such enormous benefits to be gained from exercise that unless movement is medically contraindicated (as in an acute flare-up of arthritis) the risk is worth taking. As most chronic pain is not a sign of injury, exercise poses no greater risk of damage than to a fit, healthy person. It is thought that exercise stimulates production of endorphins, enkephalins and 5-hydroxytryptamine (Sternbach, 1987) so that pain tolerance increases. Exercise may alter pathological neuropathic patterns of nerve firing by changing the input of stimuli—so closing the 'gate'. The achievement of activity and of work and leisure goals undoubtedly has a positive effect on self-confidence, control and social life. Subjects with pain in a study by Walker *et al* (1990) overwhelmingly reported that 'the worst aspect of having pain was not being able to do things'.

The safety of exercise is enhanced by the following guiding principle. Find or estimate the most movement that can be achieved, then encourage the patient to exercise at only one-third of this extent, once or twice a day. Thus exercise will not result in failure to achieve a target, will not result in fatigue which prohibits repetition of the exercise, and will not damage the structure of the body (muscles, joints and ligaments). The amount of exercise can be gradually increased as the body regains its health and strength.

There are three types of exercise, which aim to enhance strength, flexibility and endurance. *Strength* is increased by the use of isometric (same length) exercise, using muscles to push or pull against a resistance. *Flexibility* is increased by moving joints passively or actively through their range of movements. *Endurance* is increased by isotonic ('same tone') exercise, involving active movement of part or all of the body, e.g. by walking, jogging, dancing or swimming. Endurance exercises are aerobic and so improve heart and lung as well as musculo-skeletal function.

Exercise may be undertaken under the guidance of a physiother-apist, in a pain clinic, in hospital or at home, alone or with a group. First and foremost, the person with chronic pain must be convinced of the safety and desirability of this important strategy for coping with chronic pain. Books written for people in pain, such as those by Peck (1985) and Sternbach (1987), may be recommended by nurses to such people (a longer list of resources is given at the end of Chapter 9).

In summary, exercise is a distraction and a counterirritant, as well as a liberation from the potential tyranny of chronic pain.

RELAXATION

Relaxation is a state in which tension is minimal, skeletal muscle tone relaxed, pulse, respiratory rate and blood pressure lowered, and thinking calm. Sternbach (1987) suggested that 'most patients with chronic pain seem to have lost the ability to relax completely'. It is probable that many people without pain have lost this ability by the time they reach adulthood and have replaced it with leisure activities. Children and pets are generally good exemplars of relaxation.

Many non-pharmacological strategies, including some use of imagery, self-hypnosis, biofeedback, massage and warmth as well as meditative states, can produce a state of relaxation. The breaking of the cycle of muscle tension, anxiety and pain can enhance the ability to cope with pain. Paradoxically, although relaxation is a state of doing, feeling and thinking the minimum—the opposite of making an effort—mental and physical preparations are helpful and necessary, especially when learning a specific technique. For every relaxation technique, the person has to decide how to order their thoughts, their body (especially posture) and the environment (quietness). Once learned, it may be possible to relax quickly and easily even in an uncomfortable and noisy environment. Learning to relax when in pain is more difficult than learning to relax when not in pain. Therefore if pain is predicted, the relaxation technique could or should be taught beforehand. Midwives teach relaxation strategies for labour in the antenatal period. Patients can be taught prior to investigations and surgery. However, people can be helped to relax even when in pain by demonstration and guidance.

There are three techniques which require no equipment and can be learned in principle in 5–10 minutes. One is progressive muscle relaxation. This involves intentionally tensing and then relaxing the main skeletal muscles of the limbs, buttocks, abdomen, neck and face in turn. The aim is to have deeply relaxed muscles in the whole body. A comfortable sitting or lying posture and a quiet environment are helpful. Thinking is initially engaged in instructing and monitoring the body state and eventually in drifting. A second method is breathing control. Again, comfort and quiet are desirable. Thinking is concentrated first on muscular and postural relaxation, then on breathing in and out—letting tension go with each exhalation. The third method, autogenic training, is the use of a series of self-statements—relaxing ideas and visualizations, for example, of warmth and heaviness in limbs, body and head.

These three methods are biofeedback without any monitoring machinery to display the effects. They can be taught by a carer, or learned from a text or a tape recording. Nurses have many opportunities to help people use appropriate relaxation techniques, both in hospital and in the community. They are not a substitute for analgesics but are truly complementary strategies.

The goal of relaxation is not to fall asleep but to feel restored and refreshed with less tension-induced pain and more reserves to cope with life and pain. Lazarus and Folkman (1984) defined coping as 'a constantly changing cognitive and behavioural effort to manage specific external and/or internal demands that are appraised as taking or exceeding the resources of a person'. Pain, whether acute or chronic, makes insistent demands on the resources of the sufferer. Nurses can help people to choose and use these non-pharmacological strategies to manage pain, to complement pharmacological management and so to increase their resources.

CONCLUSION

It would seem that the management of pain using non-pharmacological interventions has a major part to play in the reduction of pain and suffering. The simpler cutaneous and cognitive methods are generally used by people in pain with or without the aid of professional carers. Specialized physical and psychological techniques tend to be the province of physiotherapist, psychotherapist or alternative practitioner. The extent to which nurses wish or need to gain and use these skills may depend upon their choice of career, the patient groups cared for and the skills available in teams of health professionals.

Useful texts and reviews of pain management not previously

mentioned include Tan (1982), Snyder (1984), Mehta (1986), Wall and Melzack (1989), Bonica (1990), Doody *et al* (1991) and Wells and Tschudin (1993).

REFERENCES

Barbour LA, McGuire DA & Kirchoff KR (1986) Non-analgesic methods of pain control used by cancer outpatients. *Oncology Nursing Forum* **13** (6): 56–60.

Bonica JJ (ed.) (1990) *The Management of Pain*, 2nd edn. Philadelphia: Lea & Febiger.

Buber M (1966) *The Knowledge of Man: A Philosophy of the Inter-human.* New York: Harper & Row.

Casement P (1985) *On Learning from the Patient*, p 4. London: Tavistock.

Chapman R (1984) New directions in the understanding and management of pain. *Social Science and Medicine* **19** (12): 1261–1277.

Degenaar JJ (1979) Some philosophical considerations on pain. *Pain* **7**: 281–304.

Diamond AW & Coniam SW (1991) *The Management of Chronic Pain.* Oxford University Press.

Doody SB, Smith C & Webb J (1991) Non-pharmacologic interventions for pain management. *Critical Care Nursing Clinics of North America* **3** (1): 69–75.

Duffin D (1985) Acupuncture and acupressure. In Michel TH (ed.) *Pain*, Ch. 5. International Perspectives in Physical Therapy I. Edinburgh: Churchill Livingstone.

Editorial (1982) Cooling more effective. *Aches and Pains* **3**: 37 (as quoted in McCaffery and Beebe, 1989).

Fernandez E (1986) A classification system of cognitive coping strategies of pain. *Pain* **26**: 141–151.

Fordham M (1985) *Deconditioning and reconditioning following elective surgery.* PhD Thesis, University of London.

Fordyce W (1973) An operant conditioning method for managing chronic pain. *Postgraduate Medicine* **53**: 123–128.

Flor H, Haag G, Turk DC & Koehler H (1983) Efficacy of EMG feedback, pseudotherapy and conventional medical treatment for rheumatoid back pain. *Pain* **17**: 21–31.

Friedman AM (1992) *Treating Chronic Pain. The Healing Relationship.* London: Plenum Press.

Hackett G & Horan JJ (1980) Stress inoculation for pain. What's really going on? *Journal of Counselling Psychology* **27**: 107–116.

Han J (1989) Central neurotransmitter and acupuncture analgesia. In Pomeranz B & Stux G (eds) *Scientific bases of acupuncture.* New York: Springer.

Hayward J (1991) Oral Communication to RCN Pain Forum, London.

Hildegard ER (1975) The alleviation of pain by hypnosis. *Pain* **1**: 213–231.

Illich I (1976) *Limits to Medicine. Medical Nemesis: The Exploration of Health.* Harmondsworth: Penguin.

Keefe FJ, Caldwell DS, Martinez S, Nunley J, Beckham J & Williams DA (1991) Analyzing pain in rheumatoid arthritis patients. Pain coping strategies in patients who have had knee replacement surgery. *Pain* **46**: 153–160.

LaFoy J & Geden EA (1989) Post-episiotomy pain: warm versus cold sitz baths. *Journal of Obstetrics, Gynecologic and Neonatal Nursing* **18** (5): 399–403.

Latham J (1987, 1991) Pain Control. London: Austen Cornish in association with the Lisa Sainsbury Foundation.

Lawrence DR & Bennett PN (1980) *Clinical pharmacology*, 5th edn. Edinburgh: Churchill Livingstone.

Lazarus R & Folkman S (1988) *Stress, Appraisal and Coping*. New York: Springer.

Lehmann JF (1982) *Therapeutic Heat and Cold*, 3rd edn. Baltimore: Williams & Wilkins.

Mackworth JF (1976) The development of attention. In Hamilton V & Vernon MD (eds) *The Development of Cognitive Processes*. New York: Academic Press.

Mannheimer JS (1985) TENS: uses and effectiveness. In Michel TH (ed.) *Pain*, Ch. 4. International Perspectives in Physical Therapy I. Edinburgh: Churchill Livingstone.

McCaffery M & Beebe A (1989) *Pain: Clinical Manual for Nursing Practice*. St Louis: CV Mosby.

Mehta M (1986) Current views on non-invasive methods of pain relief. In Swerdlow M (ed.) *The Therapy of Pain*, 2nd edn. pp 115–131. Massachusetts: MTP Press.

Mustafa AA & Rokke PP (1991) Can anxiety help us tolerate pain? *Pain* **46**: 43–51.

Orme MT & Dinges DF (1984) Hypnosis. In Wall PD & Melzack R (eds) *Textbook of Pain*, pp 808–816. Edinburgh: Churchill Livingstone.

Park G & Fulton B (1991) *The Management of Acute Pain*. Oxford: Oxford University Press.

Peck C (1985) *Controlling Chronic Pain. A self-help Guide*, 2nd edn. London: Fontana/Collins.

Ramler D & Roberts J (1986) A comparison of cold and warm sitz baths for relief of postpartum perineal pain. *Journal of Obstetric, Gynecologic and Neonatal Nursing* **15**: 471–474.

Richardson PH & Vincent CA (1986) Acupuncture for the treatment of pain: a review of the evaluative research. *Pain* **24**: 15–40.

Rosensteil AK & Keefe FJ (1983) The use of coping strategies in chronic low back pain patients: relationship to patient characteristics and current adjustment. *Pain* **17**: 33–44.

Russell JA (1978) Evidence of convergent validity on the dimensions of affect. *Journal of Personality and Social Psychology* **30**: 1152–1168.

Snyder M (1984) Progressive relaxation as a nursing intervention: an analysis. *Advances in Nursing Science*, April, 47–58.

Sternbach R (1987) *Mastering Pain. A Twelve-step Regimen for Coping with Chronic Pain*. London: Arlington Books.

Tan S (1982) Cognitive and cognitive–behavioural methods for pain control: a selective review. *Pain* **12**: 201–228.

Thompson JW (1986) The role of transcutaneous electrical nerve stimulation (TENS) for the control of pain. In Doyle D (ed.) *International Symposium on Pain Control*, pp 27–47. London: Royal Society of Medicine.

Turk DC & Flor H (1984) Etiological theories and treatments for chronic low back pain. II Psychological models and interactions. *Pain* **19**: 209–233.

Turner JA & Chapman CR (1982) Psychological interventions for chronic pain: a critical review. II Operant conditioning, hypnosis and cognitive behavioural therapy. *Pain* **12**: 24–46.

Whedon M & Ferrell BR (1991) Professional and ethical considerations in the use of high-tech pain management. *Oncology Nursing Forum* **18** (7): 1135–1144.

Walker JM, Akinsanya JA, Davis BD & Marcer D (1990) The nursing management of elderly patients with pain in the community: study and recommendations. *Journal of Advanced Nursing* **15**: 1154–1161.

Wall PD (1984) Summary and conclusions. In Wall PD & Melzack R (eds) *Textbook of Pain*, p 840. Edinburgh: Churchill Livingstone.

Wall P & Melzack R (eds) (1989) *Textbook of Pain*, 2nd edn. Edinburgh: Churchill Livingstone.

Wells R & Tschudin V (eds) (1993) Well's Supportive Therapies in Health Care. London: Baillière Tindall.

Williams DA & Keefe FJ (1991) Pain beliefs and the use of cognitive coping strategies. *Pain* **46**: 185–190.

Worthington Jr EL (1978) The effects of imagery content, choice of imagery content and self-verbalization of the self-control of pain. *Cognitive Therapeutic Research* **2**: 225–240.

8

Role Relationships in Pain Management

We have tried to highlight some of the knowledge, beliefs and skills that may influence the relationship of nurses with people who have pain. This chapter discusses ways in which nurses, other carers and patients may mutually affect one another's roles, thus summarizing many of the issues that have been raised earlier in the book.

The role adopted by the nurse in caring for patients in pain depends upon experience, knowledge, skill, the situation or setting, and the complementary role of others, including the person in pain, family and friends, doctors, occupational therapists, physiotherapists and psychotherapists.

Nurses can function in two apparently contrasting ways, rather as matter can behave as wave or as particle! One way in which a nurse may function is as the person who does whatever would otherwise be left undone. This nurse role is akin to a liquid which flows in and around everything—the soothing balm. In this role nursing boundaries are open. The nurse behaves in an adaptive way, being, for example, carer, friend, team leader, team player, listener, advocate, teacher or learner in turn. The other way of functioning is as a nurse specialist who is skilled in specific pain relief techniques such as massage, the use of TENS or psychotherapeutic counselling. This role is more like a solid with clear boundaries than a fluid. This nurse is called upon to use these specialist skills in specific situations and to develop, monitor and research the efficacy of particular techniques. It is increasingly possible for nurses to define their own role and acquire

₊ant specialist skills in pain therapies to the benefit of patients. ₊ıe combination of both generalist and specialist experience can enable such a nurse to be a mediator and interpreter of the pain languages of both lay and professional carers.

The potential impact of new roles on nursing is a recognized issue, evidenced by the formulation of a resolution on complementary therapies to the 1992 Royal College of Nursing (RCN) Congress (Resolution 28, Thameside and Glossop Branch, RCN Congress, Blackpool, 1992): 'That this meeting of the RCN Congress discuss the implications for nursing and the role the RCN might play in the growing trend towards the use of complementary therapies'. Should all nurses aspire to be qualified masseuses, behaviour therapists or counsellors? What do we mean by qualified? How best can the nursing profession use those who have such expertise? How is the decision to be made that such techniques when used for pain control are appropriate to the well-being of a particular patient? Will the availability of such techniques become a patient privilege or a patient right in the future? How will nurses relate to other practitioners of these skills?

The potential strength of the role of the nurse as either generalist or specialist lies in the relationship between the nurse and patient and the facing of the problem of pain together. Nurses rarely bring either scalpel or anaesthetic, so apart from the medically delegated task of analgesic or other drug administration, they have to offer themselves—head, hands and humanity.

In almost all situations nurses are part of a team of carers with different skills and opportunities to help. As pain is one of the most common reasons for individuals to seek medical aid, the overwhelming majority of surgical and medical interventions aim to remove or alleviate the causes of pain. Doctors, nurses, physiotherapists and others expend much of their time and energy in putting the patient in the best condition for the body to heal itself—in the mostly realized expectation that when healing occurs, pain will disappear. Medical and surgical techniques, radiotherapy, osteopathy and some physiotherapies aim to remove the primary cause of physical pain. Nursing non-invasive techniques more often aim to reduce or eliminate the symptom of pain and allied problems such as nausea and sleeplessness, and so remove some of the suffering which accompanies pain. When the cause is not known or cannot be removed, everyone's aim is symptom control. The role of the nurse is discussed in terms of the relationship to patients, other carers and the environment (Table 1).

Table 1. Nurse roles in caring for people in pain.

In relation to the person in pain:
   Assessor
   Preventer
   Strength lender and validator
   Supporter of patient's methods of control
   Teacher of coping strategies
   Provider of specific pain therapies

In relationship to other carers:
   Advocate and evaluator
   Team member
   Team coordinator

In relationship to the environment:
   Planner, provider or controller of
      ambient temperature
      noise
      lighting
      privacy
      bedding and furnishings

THE ROLE OF THE NURSE IN RELATION TO THE PERSON IN PAIN

Assessor

Assessment was discussed in detail in Chapter 4. The close, continuous or repeated contact between nurse and patient in hospital, other institutes or home can facilitate the assessment of pain. Nurses accompany patients as they attempt to carry out their normal activities and so have rich opportunities to assess in detail both the incidence and the effect of pain on a person's life. Assessment, in particular the exploration of patients' views of their pain and its meaning to them, in itself can be a therapeutic process akin to counselling.

Preventer of pain

The nurse, family and friends of a person in pain may carry out many activities for the patient in order to prevent the exacerbation of pain. Washing, feeding and generally reducing movement may avoid the provocation of pain. Indeed, the core of nursing care of the acutely sick consists of such actions (see also Chapter 5).

The skill to dress a wound, insert a catheter, remove sutures, position a limb, help someone out of bed, etc. without adding unnecessarily to their hurt is an attribute of expert nursing, involving sensitivity, imagination and practice.

Health visitors and occupational health nurses have responsibilities and opportunities to reduce accidental injuries and repetitive strain injuries (Huskisson and Hart, 1987) in home and work environments, so reducing consequent chronic pain incidence.

Strength lender and validator

The mere presence of another person, be it nurse or other carer, can increase the fortitude with which pain is faced (see also Chapter 2). One of Copp's patients expressed it as follows: 'Even if I have my eyes closed because the pain is so bad, I know she is there and that helps me to hold on' (Copp, 1985). Nurses can often enable the person most wanted by the patient to be present. The one thing children wanted when they were in pain was their parents (Ross and Ross, 1984). Being a 'strength lender' is an emotionally draining task, so the nurse herself may need peer support. Nurses can give or arrange respite and reassurance for other 'strength lenders' such as fathers-to-be who support their partner during labour, parents of sick children in pain, families and friends of people in chronic pain, in hospital and at home. The presence of the nurse or another person provides both a witness and a validator of pain; an ally who can corroborate and communicate the experience with the sufferer and to other people. There are many occasions when a nurse is present during an invasive medical procedure such as lumbar puncture, marrow aspiration or oesophagoscopy. The skill of the doctor and the efficacy of local anaesthesia can be enhanced by the vigilance and care of the nurse who can observe the patient and communicate verbally and non-verbally while monitoring their condition.

Supporter of patients' own methods of control

Past experiences of pain lead most people to develop tactics for tolerating or reducing present pain. In communal situations people tend to hide their spontaneous behaviours or seek permission to use their own techniques. There are three main ways in which a person may respond to or cope with the stress of pain—active cognitive coping, active behavioural coping and avoidance (Billings and Moos, 1981). Helping the pain sufferer to choose the most appropriate ways of coping, and aiding and abetting their responses (Broome, 1986), are an important part of the nurse's role.

Teacher of pain coping strategies

There are many circumstances in which nurses can teach pain coping strategies. The teaching role of the nurse includes the commitment to teach other nurses and other carers, especially family and friends. Benner (1984) makes the very important point that teaching does not consist solely of formally planned learning sessions. The main aim of teaching is to return control, power and dignity to the person in pain. The nurse can not only teach specific pain coping strategies, but also share professional knowledge. Understanding of, for example, the phenomenon of pain, the expected effects of analgesics, the duration of pain-provoking procedures and the meaning of medical and other technical terminology, may increase the patients' mastery of their own predicament and facilitate informed discussion and informed consent.

Provider of specific pain therapies

The nurse's role as provider of specific pain therapies is discussed in Chapters 6 and 7, and includes the administration of pharmacological agents and the use of non-pharmacological strategies for the prevention, elimination or reduction of pain.

THE ROLE OF THE NURSE IN RELATION TO OTHER CARERS

Other carers include professional and lay people. In some settings such as hospices and pain clinics, the acknowledged focus of care is the terminal or chronic pain of the patients or clients. In other settings, such as general hospitals, nursing homes and patients' homes, pain is not always the focal problem. No one profession has the full range of knowledge, skills or power to alleviate pain.

Advocate and evaluator

In the foreword to Latham's book *Pain Control* (Latham, 1987), Professor Wall suggested that 'of all the health professionals, nurses are in the best position to observe and to advise patients and doctors'. As one author (Fordham, 1988) wrote:

If we develop our skills in assessment and help the patient to communicate, we can fulfil our role as advocate to other team members, be they nursing colleagues or members of other professions. Three conditions are necessary for successful advocacy—firstly, a belief in the patient's communication of his/her pain experience, secondly, the sensitivity to recognise pain provoking situations, especially for those who cannot communicate verbally, and thirdly, the fostering of a multi-disciplinary approach which includes the patient.

There are innumerable opportunities for nurses to learn about the pain experience of those in their care and to evaluate the outcome of interventions. Favourable and unfavourable responses to the pain interventions of other health professionals can often be monitored by nurses, for example, the modifications of pain by analgesic, anaesthetic, radiotherapy, chemotherapy or physiotherapy.

Wall in the same foreword (Latham, 1987) made a very strong case for the nurse as evaluator, comparing this role with that of:

a research worker observing the natural history of pain, its evolution, its variability and its context for individual patients and for groups of similar patients. Those at a distance need to know what is observed.

Successful advocacy and evaluation may be achieved by the combined skills of novice and expert nurses. The novice may see clearly and the more experienced nurse may understand the significance of the observations. The clarity with which nurses communicate with each other about pain can be crucial to successful advocacy and evaluation.

Team member

Formal and semiformal teams of people with expertise in dealing with pain exist in hospices and pain clinics. The therapeutic role of pain control teams in general hospital and community settings is increasingly recognized. Traditionally anaesthetists have pioneered and headed these teams. Anaesthetists have special skills in local and regional block analgesia (Bonica, 1984) and epidural anaesthesia (Bromage, 1984), and so, along with other professional specialists such as surgeons, radiotherapists and psychologists, are able to offer potential respite for people with chronic, recalcitrant pains. Nurses who have specialized in the understanding and control of pain are members of pain control teams. Such nurses are in a position to influence policy decisions which facilitate good practice and to participate in multi-disciplinary teaching and research (White, 1985).

Team coordinator

It may not matter who coordinates the pain management of patients so long as someone does. The majority of nursing takes place in general hospitals and homes, and in these settings nurses are ideally placed to take on the role of coordinator of *ad hoc* teams of pain carers. The core of such teams is likely to comprise doctor, nurses, physiotherapist and patient, possibly with others such as family, friends, chaplain or employer. The role of coordinator is that of a central channel of communication: the person who knows what everyone else is thinking and doing about the patient's pain problem.

THE ROLE OF THE NURSE IN RELATION TO THE ENVIRONMENT

The physical environment may have a negligible or a massive effect upon the experience of pain. Many pains are directly affected by posture, pressure and movement, such that appropriate furniture, bedding and aids are crucial to their management. There are some pains, for example postherpetic neuralgia, that are triggered by the gentlest touch, breath of air or change of temperature.

The relationship between pain and the general ambience in which the person is cared for may be indirectly mediated via the emotional impact as much as the physical comfort. Tension can be heightened or mood depressed by the environment. Inappropriate lighting, temperature, noise levels and air movement may increase the suffering and the physical pain of many people. People in pain may have partly or totally lost control of their environment and be reliant upon others to provide an optimal setting.

Wainwright (1985) suggested that planners of institutional buildings tend to design for the institution rather than for the human beings who will use them. Even when the user is considered it is more often the professional worker than the patient who is consulted, added to which the internal usages of hospital buildings are often altered after commissioning such that day rooms disappear and single rooms become treatment rooms or offices. Rooms for privacy and recreation space are the first casualties in internal reorganization, and it is the patients more than the carers who suffer as a result of such changes. Provision of intermittent or continuous physical privacy can have far-reaching consequences for the person in pain. Proshansky *et al* (1970) discussed the proposition that privacy can reduce social constraint and permit behaviours which are otherwise inhibited. Vocalization, vomiting and all non-verbal responses, to pain can be expressed more fluently in private than public. Fagerhaus and Strauss (1977) noted the effect of lack of privacy on the expression of pain in open burns units thus:

> It becomes essential that pain expression be kept within reasonable limits. A patient who, without inhibition cries, screams, moans, groans and constantly complains of pain is intolerable and devastating, both for the staff and the other patients.

Some pain interventions need quietness, e.g. relaxation methods, especially in the stages of learning the techniques. Nurses have undoubted control of the immediate environment of the sick. They also have potential to influence the architecture, decor and furnishings of institutions and homes, and can refer to those with specialized knowledge of equipment such as physiotherapists and occupational therapists.

THE ROLE OF THE PATIENT

Some societies prescribe clear roles for the person with pain. Illich (1976) cited the roles of Buddha: saint, warrior and victim. Members of the Bariba culture of northern Benin and Nigeria are expected to bear pain heroically; it is considered shameful to admit to pain following accidental injury, initiation ordeals or during labour (Sargent, 1984). Craig (1978) discussed cross-cultural studies of patients in pain. There are consistencies within subcultures, but also considerable differences within particular groups. Lipton and Marbach (1984) found interethnic differences in patients' stoicism and expressiveness in response to pain. Twentieth-century psychoanalytical ideas, that failure to express responses to traumatic events at the time of their occurrence can lead to psychological problems in the future, can be extended to physical pain (Friedman, 1992). However, in our multiethnic societies we need to remember that for some individuals the consequences of admitting behaviourally or verbally that they are in pain may demoralize them far more than the pain itself.

On the whole, Western societies fail to give clear guidelines; consequently many people oscillate between the roles of hero and victim, and look to carers for clues about acceptable, appropriate behaviour. It may be courageous to attempt to deal with pain alone. It may, paradoxically, require courage to admit to pain. For example, the person who has a painful limb amputated only to suffer phantom pains may fear that their complaint may be trivialized or disbelieved. The greatest apparent heroism is displayed by those who have suffered some injury and are temporarily without pain, who are thus enabled to ignore injury and seek help in a calm way, such as by carrying a severed limb home or to hospital.

The role adopted by patients is to a certain extent determined by the carers. The conventional way of describing the behaviour of the patient with chronic or intractable pain who goes from one medical specialist to another, then to alternative or complementary practitioners, is as someone who fails to understand the nature and purpose of their pain (Pilowsky and Spence, 1976). At the least such a person is likely to be called irrational, and at worst may acquire a more pejorative psychiatric label. An holistic approach and interdisciplinary cooperation could undoubtedly reduce the need for such patient behaviour and would also help the helpers to cope with the despair of failure to remove everyone's pain (Fordham, 1988).

It is probably unwise to deny or undermine a particular role unless an alternative role can be offered which is likely to improve the outcome for the pain sufferer. This is particularly true for people with intractable pain, as they may be left defenceless and angry with a futile and helpless carer, where professional, technical pain-killing fails. Whatever label we give to the role of the patient, two major modes of behaviour—active and passive—can be distinguished. Active and passive roles are not synonyms for virtue and vice; either may be appropriate to the circumstance.

An active or passive role maybe taken by the person who is silent about pain and chooses to deal with their pain alone. Such a person may actively use internally focused methods of pain control, such as vigilant focusing, mind–body separation, or fantasy; externally focused methods such as 'flight into activity' and seeking companions; or use passive avoidance strategies such as posture, stillness or sleep. Copp (1974) reported that, out of 100 interviewees, some with acute and some with chronic pain, most used both cognitive and behavioural strategies. Children used similar strategies to adults. An extreme passive role is taken by those who wish to depend solely on other people, their drugs, surgery, etc. to obliterate pain. The more common role of the patient in pain is a mixture of active and passive participation in cooperation with professional carers.

The role adopted may or may not be helpful. Whether a person plays an active or passive role in dealing with acute pain will possibly have little effect on the long-term outcome, as such pains disappear when healing is complete. The transfer or loss of control and the abdication of self-responsibility are inevitable and helpful at times of great need, such as when the prolongation of severe pain would have dangerous consequences. However, people with chronic intermittent or intractable pain may have to unlearn a dependent role and struggle to regain independence and control of their own lives if they are to live successfully despite pain. Coping with chronic pain is typified as an active process by Walker *et al* (1989, 1990) 'in which an individual's predictions of being able to control a situation is influenced by perceptions of all current events, and influenced by available information, past experiences and controlling skills or action' (Walker *et al*, 1990).

ROLES IN THE COMMUNITY

Certain issues are heightened when people receive care in their own homes. Many of these issues arise as a result of chronic pain which presents a set of adaptive tasks that do not arise when the patient experiences pain management in the hospital. A shift in roles occurs, which creates new responsibilities for patients and their families.

First, a major difference between care at home and care in the hospital is that the patient assumes many of the tasks of the therapeutic plan that are usually done by doctors and nurses. These include, for example, administering treatments (including medications), monitoring effects and identifying when a change in pain or the appearance of side-effects requires re-evaluation and a change in the therapeutic plan. When the patient goes home from hospital the responsibility for these tasks is transferred; unfortunately, far too often this shift in responsibility is not made explicit, and the knowledge and skills needed to manage the tasks effectively are not passed on. Thus, one major nursing activity when working with patients at home is to ensure that they possess the knowledge and skills to assume, safely and effectively, the responsibilities that have been handed over upon discharge. Moreover, for patients to carry out confidently the activities of the therapeutic plan, informed support must be accessible to them. Questions that should be explicitly addressed at the time of discharge are: who is available to help? How does the patient get in touch with them? How do patients communicate their concerns? It is also helpful to provide a written copy of the requisite information, since the flurry of activity that accompanies discharge and the anxiety about going home often makes it difficult for patients to remember details.

A second issue that is peculiar to pain management at home is the problem of finding a place for it in the life of the patient. This may require adaptations in two areas. First, the patient must incorporate the therapeutic plan into their usual routines. They must remember, for example, to take regularly scheduled medication, or work out how to structure the day to include two 10-minute sessions of relaxation. Secondly, the patient must, as Strauss and his colleagues noted, 'normalize the interactions with others and their style of life' (Strauss *et al*, 1984). When patients are in the hospital, life is interrupted. Usual family activities, roles and relationships are suspended for a time. The suspension, however, cannot continue indefinitely and when the patient is discharged home, normal life must be taken up again.

Sometimes this is easily accomplished, but some patients may find that there are changes to be negotiated. These may involve practical issues such as obtaining equipment or supplies that were routinely available in hospital but are not available at home. The patient may not be able to return to full-time work and may have pressing financial concerns. Other adaptations may have to do with the development of ways to accommodate changes in functioning that result from the continued pain or its treatment. Because of the interactive nature of families, these changes, while primarily affecting the patient, will create demands at some level for the other family members. Therefore both the patient and the family may have to rethink their roles.

REFERENCES

Benner P (1984) *From Novice to Expert. Excellence and Power in Clinical Nursing Practice*. Menlo Park: Addison-Wesley.

Billings G & Moos RH (1981) The role of coping responses and social resources in attenuating the stress of life events. *Journal of Behavioural Medicine* **4** (2): 139–157.

Bonica JJ (1984) Local anaesthesia and regional blocks. In Wall PD & Melzack R (eds) *Textbook of Pain*, Ch. 1. Edinburgh: Churchill Livingstone.

Bromage PR (1984) Epidural anaesthetics and narcotics. In Wall PD & Melzack R (eds) *Textbook of Pain*. Edinburgh: Churchill Livingstone.

Broome A (1986) Coping with pain. Strategies for relief. *Nursing Times* April 16: 43–44.

Copp LA (1974) The spectrum of suffering. *American Journal of Nursing* **79** (3): 491–495.

Copp LA (1985) Pain coping. *Perspectives of Pain, Recent Advances in Nursing 11*. Ch. 1. Edinburgh: Churchill Livingstone.

Craig KD (1978) Social modelling influences on pain. In Sternbach RA (ed.) *The Psychology of Pain*. New York: Academic Press.

Fagerhaus SY & Strauss A (1977) *Politics of Pain Management: staff–patient interactions*. Menlo Park: Addison-Wesley.

Friedman AM (1992) *Treating Chronic Pain: The Healing Partnership.* London: Plenum Press.

Fordham M (1988) Pain. In Wilson-Barnett J & Batehup L (eds) *Patient Problems. A Research Base for Nursing Care,* Ch. 8. London: Scutari Press.

Huskisson EC & Dudley Hart F (1987) *Joint Disease and the Arthropathies.* Bristol: Wright.

Illich I (1976) *Limits to Medicine. Medical Nemesis: The Expropriation of Health.* Harmandsworth: Penguin.

Latham J (1987) Foreword by Professor P Wall. *Pain Control.* Reading: Austin Cornish in association with the Lisa Sainsbury Foundation.

Lipton JA & Marbach JJ (1984) Ethnicity and the pain experience. *Social Science and Medicine* **19** (12): 1279–1298.

Pilowsky I & Spence ND (1976) Illness behaviour syndromes associated with intractable pain. *Pain* **2**: 61–71.

Proshansky HM, Ittleson WH & Rivlin LG (1970) *Environmental Psychology.* New York: Holt Rinehart & Winston.

Ross DM & Ross SA (1984) Childhood pain: the school-aged child's viewpoint. *Pain* **20**: 179–191.

Sargent C (1984) Between death and shame: dimensions of pain in Bariba culture. *Social Science and Medicine* **19** (12): 1299–1304.

Strauss AL, Corbin J, Fagerhaugh S, Glaser BG, Maines D, Suczek B & Wiener CL (1984) *Chronic Illness and the Quality of Life,* 2nd edn, p 16. St Louis: CV Mosby.

Wainwright P (1985) Impact of hospital architecture on the patient in pain. In Copp LA (ed.) *Perspectives on Pain. Recent Advances in Nursing,* Ch. 4. Edinburgh: Churchill Livingstone.

Walker JM, Akinsanja JA, Davis BD & Marcer D (1989) The nursing management of pain in the community: a theoretical framework. *Journal of Advanced Nursing* **14** (3): 240–247.

Walker JM, Akinsanja JA, Davis BD & Marcer D (1990) The nursing management of elderly patients with pain in the community: study and recommendations. *Journal of Advanced Nursing* **15**: 1154–1161.

White R (1985) Policy implications and constraint in the role of the nurse in the management of pain. In Copp LA (ed.) *Perspectives on Pain, Recent Advances in Nursing.* Ch. 6. Edinburgh: Churchill Livingstone.

9

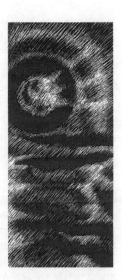

Concluding Thoughts on Nursing People in Pain

In our discussion of the issues surrounding the care of people in pain we have noted that the definition of pain is itself an issue. No one definition will do, except perhaps the comprehensive one of the National Institutes of Health given on p 38. The working definition of pain by McCaffery (1972) is most useful when caring for conscious people with whom we can converse (see pages 7 and 24). The categorical labelling of pain is also an issue. Classification of pain has not achieved the clarity of, for example, botanical naming. An annual, biennial or perennial plant can be defined *a priori*; botanists do not have to wait for the first, alternate or subsequent years of persistent survival. By contrast, an acute pain may be redefined as a chronic pain if it persists, though the nature of the pain may or may not have altered.

The point of classification is to facilitate communication. Additional ways of classifying pain are by site (e.g. head, joint, heart, pelvis) or by pathology if known (e.g. malignant, non-malignant, inflammatory or ischaemic). Labels do not tell us all that we need to know about pain and can even be misleading if we think they can inform us about the intensity or nature of the experience of the person in pain. A non-malignant pain may well be malign; a headache such as migraine may be more severe than a cancer pain. Labels are a form of shorthand; we need to check with one another that we share the longhand when we use them. For instance, McCaffery and Beebe used the shorthand term 'chronic non-malignant pain' to stand for 'pain that has lasted 6 months or longer, is ongong on a daily basis, is due to non-life-threatening causes, has not responded to currently available treatment methods, and may continue for the remainder of the patient's life' (McCaffery and Beebe, 1989, p 232). See Chapter 3 for other definitions.

If a major impact is to be made on the prevalence of pain, ways of preventing the onset of chronic intractable pains must be found. Current theories about pain and pain treatment, whether physiological or psychological, are fairly good at describing and explaining but not so good at predicting.

NURSING

Nursing is at the interface of conventional medicine, complementary therapies and common sense; not an easy place to be, and one requiring insight, creativity and flexibility. Being alongside people in pain means learning from patients what pain means to them, what goals they wish to achieve, what interventions they find acceptable and useful, and empowering them by sharing information and strategy skills.

The ethical issue of enabling people to give informed consent as opposed to uninformed consent should be rephrased as informed *choice*. We can help patients in pain to make decisions and take action for themselves by the provision of information. A list of information sources (books, a videotape and an audiotape cassette) designed for people in pain is included at the end of this chapter. If we use these sources and recommend them to our patients, we go some way to empowering people in pain.

The importance of nursing is acknowledged in a statement by Wall (1989)

> Most treatments (for pain) remain pragmatic, as with aspirin and opium, or from ancient common sense and humanity, as in nursing care, distraction, massage, heat, cold, structural support, rest and encouragement.

Nursing is concerned with the control of a symptom as part of the total care of a person. In *Defeating Pain*, Wall and Jones (1991) characterized the centrality of caring and symptom control as follows:

> People in pain and those who care for them are . . . rising up in revolt against their passive waiting until a cure appears. One reaction is to search the classical folk remedies abandoned by modern medicine. Another reaction is to demand better day-to-day care of the patient, which is another way of describing control of symptoms, principally pain.

A dilemma which has exercised health professionals and the public recently is whether we should use strategies (particularly so-called complementary ones) if we do not know if or how they work. The overwhelming need of people for pain relief is such that it is as unethical to withhold a method of treatment because we are unsure of how it works as it is to use a method that has iatrogenic side-effects which outweigh the benefits. The issue is discussed by Buckman and Sabbagh (1993).

Has the nursing care of people with pain improved over the generations? It is difficult to answer this question. So much has changed in the practice of medicine and nursing and the experience of patients in the last few decades. Knowledge, skills and technological advances have increased the scope of surgical and medical interventions. Undoubtedly people are surviving formerly fatal conditions. Does this mean there is more or less pain around? Abu Saad (1984) suggests that there is more. Prior to 1965 gate control theory had not been proposed, but the core of nursing consisted of comfort measures such as 4-hourly massage and movement of anyone who was in bed for more than 12 hours; the use of hot and cold applications for aches, pains and inflammation, including warm hot-water bottles, ice packs and poultices. The massage of pressure areas over bony prominences is not of course the same as massage of soft tissue—but did it reduce pain? Nurses inevitably spent much time in close physical contact with or proximity to patients, and stayed full-time with ('specialled') any seriously ill person who today would be cared for in an intensive care or other high-technology unit. There was no technology at the bedside to distract nurses from their care of the patient.

One conclusion that can be drawn from these rather selective reminiscences is that when we change the practices of nursing for what seem to be valid reasons, e.g. shortening hours of work, changing the skill mix, abandoning pressure area massage and the use of hot-water bottles (at least in many institutions), or shorten the length of time people stay in bed and stay in hospital, we need to evaluate what is lost as well as what is gained, and if possible compensate for any losses.

When contact time with patients is short, assessment of pain has to be achieved efficiently. To the extent that community care necessarily places a greater onus on patient self-responsibility and on family and friends as carers, the importance of teaching and empowering potential pain sufferers increases (Seers, 1990).

There are some heartening findings. For example, Fothergill-Bourbonnais and Wilson-Barnett (1992) found that more nurses knew the minimal risk of addiction from analgesic use for pain than was the case in previously cited studies; and in a study by Walker *et al* (1990) the majority of elderly patients with chronic pain reported that they were coping fairly well and placed great emphasis on the supportive role of the district nurse.

However, there is no doubt that we could do much better at preventing or at least reducing the pain of children (Eland, 1985; Ross and Ross, 1988; Gillies, 1993), as well as reducing acute postoperative pain for all ages (Seers, 1987; Closs *et al*, 1993). Brief iatrogenic pains can be and often are forestalled by good medical and nursing practice. Many strategies for reducing the impact of chronic pains are within the scope of nursing. A role that could perhaps be more positively developed is that of preventing some of the psychosocial morbidity of some chronic pain sufferers.

ASSESSMENT

Unless we attempt to see pain through the eyes of the sufferer we are unlikely to take appropriate decisions and actions to help. A good deal of knowledge about assessment exists but seems not always to be used. Nash *et al* (1993) made three points arising from nursing research studies about this gap between available knowledge and practice:

1. Nurses' assessments do not always match patients' own assessments.
2. Nurses tend to infer less pain than is actually being experienced— see Seers (1987) for example.
3. Nurses' documentation of pain assessments typically contains minimal amounts of information compared with that available from the patient (Camp and O'Sullivan, 1987).

In a study of district nurses (Walker *et al*, 1990) only 18 instances out of 146 responses reported using a formal pain assessment protocol. The researchers concluded, however, that 'there is limited utility in measuring persistent pain in isolation from other related factors; it is the impact on the patient's life that matters. Agreed—but is there something wrong with existing assessment formats, or were these nurses unaware of the more comprehensive tools and those designed for community use? Perhaps we need to examine critically the impact of assessment formats on nurses and nursing. The nursing assessment of pain is acknowledged to be much broader than the assessment of pain *per se* and many, although not all, of the assessment protocols do include aspects of the impact of pain on the sufferer (see Chapter 4). Nurses often know far more than their documentation reveals. Care studies such as those on pages 145–152, demonstrate the full, rich understanding of the nurses.

The format of nursing care planning based on patient problems tends to compartmentalize the person into a number of apparently discrete parts or symptoms—a view antithetical to holism. If pain is divorced from other problems and the lifestyle of the person, care may not be holistic. Analysis and synthesis are complementary processes in the planning of care, and problems need to be cross-referenced. Being alongside somone with pain implies taking seriously whatever is the focal issue for them. It may be that if we take any patient problem seriously we will inevitably encompass their pain, as pain impinges on all aspects of living if it persists.

INTERVENTIONS

It is comparatively easy to decide in broad terms what are desirable, potentially helpful nursing actions. It is the conversion of the general into the particular that is difficult. It might be helpful to use the reasearch of Kitson *et al* (1993) into the development of criteria for postoperative pain management in two ways—as a guide to methods of producing criteria and as a source of published criteria. The first eight of the expert-derived process criteria are interactions between nurse and surgical patient which can, could or should occur prior to surgery. They include exploring the patient's history of pain, their coping methods and experience of pain relief, and the teaching of coping strategies. Criterion lists cannot prescribe the content of such nursing but remind us that if we first find out what a person already knows and what they want to know, we can tailor our actions, including teaching, to individual needs. We cannot tell a person how much pain they will experience, but we can plan and teach ways to avoid, reduce or cope with pain *before* it occurs rather than *when* it occurs. For example, if patient-controlled analgesia is a postoperative option the person should be taught how to use it before the operation if possible not when recovering from anaesthesia. We cannot know in advance how much of the prescribed drug will be desired by any individual; wide variations in need have been reported by researchers (Bennett *et al*, 1982; Lehmann *et al*, 1990; Shade, 1992).

Current nursing research is providing many guidelines for practice. For example, the list of potential interventions which intensive therapy and hospice nurses cited as contributing to pain relief in the study by Fothergill-Bourbonnais and Wilson-Barnett (1992) could be used as an *aide-mémoire* for strategies of helping both acute and chronic pain sufferers. The flow diagram of questions and nursing interventions compiled by Walker *et al* (1990) provides a rational basis for managing the chronic pain of elderly people in the community.

CONCLUSION

We hope that readers of this book will have gained some helpful ideas and will be provoked to think about some of the issues surrounding the care of people in pain, and reflect on practice.

Copp (1993), in discussion of the nurse's responsibility for pain management, remarked:

> Although most nurses with whom we have talked have a commitment to pain reduction, far fewer work for alleviation. Pain prevention seems to fail to inspire nurses to imaginative nursing care and pain management.

The idea of preventing pain needs some unravelling. It requires at least three riders:

1. Is it what the fully informed patient wishes?
2. Is it within the gift of the caring professions?
3. Can it be achieved without incurring unacceptable side-effects?

If these three conditions are fulfilled, skilled nursing could be characterized as ensuring (in cooperation with all team members) that the person with tractable pain is *not in* pain, and the person with intractable pain is neither physically nor psychologically abandoned.

REFERENCES

Abu Saad H (1984) Assessing children's responses to pain. *Pain* **19**: 163–171.
Bennett RL, Baumann TJ & Batenhorst RL (1982) Morphine titration in postoperative laparotomy patients using patient-controlled analgesia. *Current Therapeutic Research* **32**: 45–52.
Buckman R & Sabbagh K (1993) *Magic or Medicine*. An investigation into healing. London: Macmillan.
Camp L & O'Sullivan P (1987) Comparison of medical, surgical and oncology

patients' descriptions of pain and nurses' documentation of pain assessments. *Journal of Advanced Nursing* 12: 593–598.

Closs SJ, Fairclough HL, Tierney AJ & Currie CT (1993) Pain in elderly orthopaedic patients. *Journal of Clinical Nursing* 2: 41–45.

Copp LA (1993) Guest editorial. An ethical responsibility for pain management. *Journal of Advanced Nursing* 18: 1–3.

Eland JM (1985) The role of the nurse in children's pain. In Copp LA (ed.) *Perspectives on Pain. Recent Advances in Nursing II.* Edinburgh: Churchill Livingstone.

Fothergill-Bourbonnais F & Wilson-Barnett J (1992) A comparative study of intensive care unit and hospice nurses' knowledge on pain management. *Journal of Advanced Nursing* 17: 362–372.

Gillies ML (1993) Post-operative pain in children: A review of the literature. *Journal of Clinical Nursing* 2: 5–10.

Kitson A, Harvey G, Hyndman S & Yerrell P (1993) A comparison of expert- and practitioner-derived criteria for post-operative pain management. *Journal of Advanced Nursing* 18: 218–232.

Lehmann KA, Ribbert N & Horrichs-Hayermeyer G (1990) Postoperative patient-controlled-analgesia with alfentanil: analgesic efficacy and minimal effective concentration. *Journal of Pain and Symptom Management* 5 (4): 249–258.

Mander R (1992) The control of pain in labour. *Journal of Clinical Nursing* 1: 219–223.

McCaffery M (1972) *Nursing Management of the Patient in Pain.* Philadelphia: JB Lippincott.

McCaffery M & Beebe A (1989) *Pain. Clinical Manual for Nursing Practice.* St Louis: CV Mosby.

Nash R, Edwards H & Nebauer M (1993) Effects of attitudes, subjective norms and perceived control on nurses' intention to asesss patients' pain. *Journal of Advanced Nursing* 18: 941–947.

Ross DM & Ross SA (1988) *Childhood Pain.* Baltimore: Urban & Schwarzenberg.

Seers K (1987a) Pain, anxiety and recovery in patients undergoing surgery. PhD Thesis, University of London.

Seers K (1987b) Perceptions of pain. *Nursing Times* 83: 37–39.

Seers K (1990) Early discharge after surgery; its effects on patients, their informal carers and on the workload of health professionals. *Royal College of Nursing*, Daphne Heald Research Unit, Unit Report.

Shade P (1992) Patient-controlled analgesia: can client education improve outcomes? *Journal of Advanced Nursing* 17: 408–413.

Walker JM, Akinsanya JA, Davis BD & Marcer D (1990) The nursing management of elderly patients with pain in the community: study and recommendations. *Journal of Advanced Nursing* 15: 1154–1161.

Wall PD (1989) In Wall P & Melzack R (eds) *Textbook of Pain*, 2nd edn. Edinburgh: Churchill Livingstone.

Wall PD & Jones M (1991) *Defeating Pain. The War Against a Silent Epidemic*, p 20. London: Plenum Press.

SOURCES OF INFORMATION FOR PATIENTS

Books
Broome A & Jellicoe H (1987) *Living with Pain: Self-help Guide to Managing Pain.* Leicester: British Psychological Society/Methuen.

Catalano EM (1987) The Chronic Pain Control Workbook: A Step-by-step Guide for Coping With and Overcoming Your Pain. Oakland: New Harbinger.

Melzack R & Wall PD (1991) *The Challenge of Pain.* Harmondsworth: Penguin.
A book for lay or professional people who wish to understand pain.

Peck C (1985) *Controlling Chronic Pain. A Self-help Guide.* Glasgow: Fontana/Collins.
Explains chronic pain and its consequences and gives advice on how to avoid pain, how to resume normal activity and deal with depression and relational problems in family, work and leisure.

Shone N (1992) *Coping Successfully with Pain.* London: Sheldon Press.

Sternbach R (1987) *Mastering Pain. A Twelve-step Regimen for Coping with Chronic Pain.* London: Arlington Books.
Explains pain, the problems it provokes and methods of physical, psychological and analgesic control. Helps empower the person with pain in his or her relationships with others including doctors.

Tapes
Walton Hospital Pain Relief Clinic, Liverpool (1993) *Coping with Pain.* Tape cassette produced by Magnus Magnusson and Simon Weston; includes relaxation techniques and exercises to stimulate the body's natural pain-killers. Available from Pain Tape, PO Box 1, Wirral L47 7DD.

Royal College of Nursing (1991) *Patients in Control: Patient Controlled Analgesia* (video). London: Health Care Productions.

Care Studies

Care Study 1   Postoperative Pains
Pain assessment by Melissa Clough, undergraduate student nurse, 1990

Mrs V. is a 73-year-old lady who was admitted to hospital 10 weeks ago for a colostomy formation, as part of her colon was removed due to cancer. She made quite a slow recovery post surgery and now her participation in her stoma and colostomy care varies from day to day; some days she is fully independent as regards her colostomy care, and others she appears disinterested, resists participation and barely acknowledges her stoma site. Mrs V. has a 78-year-old husband at home who is registered blind and is thus usually quite dependent on her. He is at present 'managing' with help from friends and neighbours. Mrs V. is understandably concerned about him and is thus anxious to return home. The shared goal for Mrs V. and the staff on this ward is for Mrs V. to show consistently that she is able to care for her colostomy totally independently, including cleaning of the stoma site and changing of colostomy bags, before discharging her. Mrs V. is not particularly mobile and has had a DVT in her right leg in the past.

This particular afternoon the nurse during report stated that Mrs V. appeared withdrawn and refused to participate in her colostomy care. Apparently she had been 'quiet, withdrawn and uninterested' for most of the previous week. No reasons for this were suggested and no mention was made of Mrs V. experiencing any pain. At approximately 2 p.m. I was walking down the ward to introduce myself to my patients when I walked past Mrs V. My attention was drawn to her primarily because she was moaning. I then noticed that she was hunched over her legs rocking back and forth, grimacing and at the same time rubbing her legs. Pain, like any other human experience, is capable of expression in three major ways, that is by physiological response, by behavioural response and by verbal description. Along with what I had learnt in report about Mrs V.'s quiet, withdrawn state, these behaviour responses appeared to be a very clear expression of pain. I sat down next to Mrs V. and asked her how she was feeling, to which she replied, 'I'm in agony', and added that she'd been in pain more or less continually for the past two days.

I decided to assess Mrs V.'s pain using a visual analogue scale. I asked her to rate her pain on a continuum which began at 0, representing no pain, and ended at 10, which represented the worst pain she could imagine. I chose this assessment tool for several reasons, perhaps the most important being that it is very quick and simple to use. Mrs V. appeared very agitated as a result of her pain and I felt that it was unlikely that she would be able to concentrate on anything for longer than a few seconds. This tool thus seemed most sensible as the patient doesn't even have to focus on a piece of paper. I felt that the observation chart as used by the London Hospital would have been far too complicated at this time and therefore liable to produce inaccurate results. A long questionnaire was simply not appropriate or acceptable until some measure of relief had been obtained for the pain.

Prior to intervention, Mrs V. rated her pain as 9. A brief look at her drug chart showed that the only prescribed drug for pain relief was paracetamol, a mild analgesic, as required. This had last been given 6 hours previously. Having established that Mrs V. was obviously in a lot of pain I felt that my priority was to offer her some analgesic. She said that she did want some paracetamol and so two 500 mg tablets were given. I then returned to Mrs V. to try to formulate a clearer picture of the extent and nature of the pain she was experiencing. I already knew that she had had the pain for 2 days; from further discussion I learnt that it became more unbearable in the evenings and at night usually keeping her awake. The pain was worse when she was left sitting in her chair for long periods of time. Thus it may have been that pressure was contributing to her total pain experience and thus relieving some pressure may relieve some pain. Also the fact that Mrs V. had had a previous DVT meant that she had been instructed to sit with her legs elevated. However, she was usually left for long periods with her ankles resting on a very hard footstool. She found this very uncomfortable, and experienced 'stiff, cramp-like, agonizingly sore' legs. I would have liked to have used a body outline (front and back) to reveal the extent and location of her pain. However, she was at the time, I felt, too absorbed by the pain to concentrate on doing this. To reduce the stiffness in her legs I suggested to Mrs V. that when her pain was better controlled it might be a good idea for her to try to walk a short distance, such as the width of the ward and back, every hour. I also put a pillow on the top of the footstool so that her ankles were more comfortable and explained to her that although indeed it was important for her to keep her legs elevated, if they became unbearably stiff and uncomfortable she could take them down until they felt better.

I discussed with Mrs V. what her own goal was regarding her pain and she stated that if possible she would like to be pain-free, especially at night, but if not for the pain to be maintained at a level at which she could just tolerate it. Relating back to the visual analogue scale, Mrs V. decided that this would be a rating of no higher than 3. Half an hour after the administration of analgesics I again asked Mrs V. to rate her pain on the scale. The rating she gave me was 7; however, her behavioural responses did not indicate to me that her pain had improved even this slight amount. On further questioning it came out that Mrs V. had almost felt obliged to tell me her pain had improved: 'Well, you see, you're the first one who's taken any notice and you did try your best so I didn't want to disappoint you'. However, she did keep stressing that although the pain hadn't improved that much she did feel 'stronger' and more able to cope: 'it does feel sort of better now I know you realize I've got a problem with it'. It seemed almost as if I had validated her suffering.

At this point I asked Mrs V. if she felt able to indicate her pain sites to me on a body outline, which she did. I also asked her if she could think of any words to describe her pain. The pain in her legs she described as 'nagging', 'cramping' and 'aching'. To describe the pain around her stoma site she used the words 'tender' and 'sore'. Over the next hour, although Mrs V.'s pain improved slightly to a level of 6—when her husband was visiting and she was thus more relaxed and temporarily distracted—neither of us felt that this was adequate, and so armed with the information I had gathered I went to discuss Mrs V.'s problem with sister and the doctor. From this, two decisions were made, the first being that paracetamol alone was not a suitable analgesic for Mrs V. as it obviously had little effect; it was decided that co-dydramol (dihydrocodeine tartrate 10 mg, paracetamol 500 mg) should be tried instead. Secondly, it was decided that in Mrs V.'s case the avoidance of breakthrough pain was an important aim in her pain control. For this reason it was felt that regular, not 'as necessary' (p.r.n.), prescription and administration of analgesic would be more successful in controlling her continuous pain. Also, it was clearly evident that Mrs V. was reluctant to ask for an analgesic herself even if she felt she needed it. Thus, co-dydramol was prescribed at 4-hourly intervals, to be started at 6 p.m. I explained to Mrs V. that the new plan was not just to reduce her pain but also to try and prevent it; she agreed with the new regimen.

When I was doing the drug round at 6 p.m. I noticed that Mrs V. again looked very upset and appeared to be in pain. She was alone as her husband had just popped out to eat. At this point Mrs V. again rated her pain as 9. The newly prescribed analgesic was given and I also tried to make Mrs V. more comfortable with pillows. An hour later I asked Mrs V. to reassess her pain level. She rated it as 3. She also reassessed her pain sites on the body outline and it was clear that the majority of her pain had been relieved. She was visibly more relaxed; she was more alert and chatty, much more cheerful (as pointed out by her delighted husband) and she asked me if I'd walk her out to the toilet instead of bringing the commode as usual. When I took Mrs V. to the toilet she was more cooperative and actually expressed an interest in her colostomy site: 'If this pain stays away like this I might have a go at changing my own bag tomorrow'. At 8.30 p.m. Mrs V. still rated her pain as 3 and by the time I left the ward she had fallen asleep.

I felt that in the case of Mrs V. the pain assessment tools used were valuable in measuring the effectiveness of the nursing interventions used to improve her pain. Prior to using these tools I don't think that the full extent of Mrs V.'s pain was realized—it gave us a much clearer understanding of the nature and extent of her pain. The use of front and back body outlines clearly defined the extent and location of her pain. Thus, together, these tools alerted the medical staff to a problem, gave a guide as to the level of pain, indicating the appropriate level of analgesia, and finally, reassured Mrs V. that a very real problem was being taken seriously and dealt with appropriately. This in itself allowed Mrs V. a measure of control which raised her self-esteem and appeared to make her more alert and cooperative.

However, I did also feel that some difficulties arose from the use of pain assessment tools. When Mrs V. was in extreme pain it was still difficult to focus her attention even on such a simple pain rating scale because she was so agitated and overwhelmed by pain. I also think it is important to note that at times I did not feel Mrs V. was expressing her pain truthfully. Indeed, stoicism is seen as a positive virtue in many cultures, and along with this Mrs V.'s desperate goal was to return home to be with her husband and she felt that to admit any pain

Time	Pain rating	Intervention
14:00	9	Analgesic (2 paracetamols)
14:30	7	Further discussion concerning the pain. Made feet more comfortable - pillow on footstool. Body outline used, pain described:
15:30	6	Distraction/relaxation techniques employed-chatting to husband
18:00	9	Patient sitting alone-husband gone to eat. Analgesic (2 co-dydramol) Patient made more comfortable with pillows
19:00	3	Chatting with husband. Body outlines used to assess effectiveness of analgesic

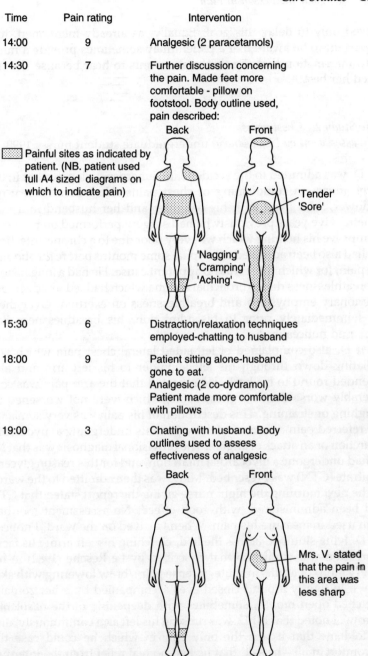

Painful sites as indicated by patient. (NB. patient used full A4 sized diagrams on which to indicate pain)

Back   Front

'Tender'
'Sore'

'Nagging'
'Cramping'
'Aching'

Back   Front

Mrs. V. stated that the pain in this area was less sharp

Short walk to toilet

Figure 1. *Summary of pain management.*

served only to delay this goal. Equally, as already mentioned, it is important to be aware that a patient may sometimes provide a nurse with information that she thinks she wants to hear because she has 'tried her best'.

Care Study 2   Chest pains
Pain assessment by Lisa Manley, undergraduate student nurse, 1990

Mr D. was admitted to the accident and emergency department in the early afternoon complaining of chest pains. He was a 73-year-old widower, who lived with his daughter and her husband in a maisonette. Five years previously he had surgery performed on both ears to improve his hearing which was very poor due to a chronic infection. He had also been admitted to hospital some months before for abdominal pain, for which there was no apparent cause. He had a long history of breathlessness due to bronchial asthma which had led to a degree of pulmonary emphysema and breathlessness on exertion. Over the 2 days immediately prior to his admission, his breathlessness had increased noticeably.

Mr D. also complained of left-sided lateral chest pain which was radiating down through his left shoulder to his left arm and also extended round to his back. He reported that the arm pain was considerably worse than his chest pains, which were not worsened by coughing or straining. This description of his pain was very similar to the referred pain commonly felt by patients undergoing a myocardial infarction or an attack of angina. The provisional diagnosis was that Mr D. had undergone a myocardial infarction, and for this reason glyceryl trinitrate (GTN) was prescribed. Mr D. was then admitted to the ward.

The next morning the night nurse giving the report stated that GTN had been administered 'with good effect'. No assessment tool had been used to measure his pain. When I arrived on the ward, I noticed Mr D. lying slumped across the bed, clutching his left arm. His facial expression was similar to that described by Le Resche (1982) in his observations of adults in acute, intense pain; 'brow lowering with skin drawn in tightly around closed eyes accompanied by a horizontally stretched open mouth, sometimes with deepening of the nasolabial furrow'. I noted that Mr D. was rubbing his left arm continuously, and he told me that it was the only way in which he could ease the discomfort at all—he said that he had no real relief from the intermittent recurrent episodes of 'needling, nagging' pain for more than 2 days.

I decided to assess Mr D.'s pain using a visual analogue scale. I asked Mr D. to rate his pain on a continuum from 0 (no pain) to 10 (the worst pain you could imagine). I decided to use this assessment tool for several reasons, the most important being that it is extremely quick and simple to use. It does not require a piece of paper that the patient has to focus on. In my opinion Mr D. was unable to concentrate on anything for longer than a few seconds. I felt that the observation chart as used by the London Hospital would have been far too complex for Mr D. to use at this time, and therefore that the results would not have been accurate.

Mr D. rated his pain as being 7 before any intervention was carried out. I obtained some GTN tablets for him, as this was the only drug prescribed. However, 15 minutes later, when I asked Mr D. to reassess his pain and the rating remained 7, I realized that had the pain been due to angina, the relief would have been almost immediate. On the basis of this, a doctor re-examined the patient, and noting the limited flexion and rotation of the arm, decided that the pain could have been due to a trapped cervical nerve. He prescribed indomethacin, a non-steroidal anti-inflammatory drug, and co-dydramol, a compound analgesic preparation containing dihydrocodeine tartrate and par-acetamol. Mr D. was also seen by the physiotherapist who advised that in order to relieve pain, Mr D. should either sit on the bed, leaning forward over the bedside table, leaning on two pillows, or sit upright in bed, with back, neck and head well supported by four or five pillows.

Indomethacin and co-dydramol were administered, and Mr D. was helped to sit in the position that had been recommended. An hour later, I asked Mr D. to reassess his pain level. He rated it as 3. He had visibly relaxed, his eyes were open, and he was able to communicate with much greater ease. He was starting to take an interest in things around him, and decided that after lunch he would have a wash and a shave.

I asked Mr D. what his own goal was for his pain problem, and he replied that he wanted to be free of the pain if possible and if not, to maintain it at a level of 3 or below. This too was the nursing goal.

The pain level did not increase until after 4 p.m. The physiotherapist had returned with a cervical support collar for Mr D.; however, this did not help his pain, and within half an hour, his pain had increased dramatically to 7. The collar was removed and the pain decreased to 4. However, this did not fulfil either Mr D.'s goal or the nursing goal. At this point, Mr D.'s relatives arrived, and in their company he seemed to relax. After they left he rated his pain level as 3. However, the analgesia began to wear off shortly afterwards and by 6 p.m. his pain had increased to 6. Co-dydramol and indomethacin were again administered and an hour later his pain had decreased once more to 3. It stayed at this level at 8.30 p.m., and by 9 p.m. Mr D. had fallen asleep (Table 1).

Table 1. Mr D.'s pain assessed on a visual analogue scale.

Time	Pain Rating	Intervention
0900	7	GTN tablet
0915	7	Different position
		Analgesic (co-dydramol)
		Anti-inflammatory drug (indomethacin)
1100	3	Distraction techniques employed, e.g. chatting to other people, reading newspaper, sleeping
1600	3	Cervical support collar
1630	7	Collar removed
1700	4	Distraction techniques—chatting to relatives
1730	3	
1800	6	Analgesics (co-dydramol) and indomethacin
1900	3	
2030	3	

I considered that the pain rating scale was very useful in this case of acute pain: I felt that Mr D.'s pain had been neglected and ignored to a certain extent before the pain scale was implemented. This assessment tool had three benefits: firstly, it helped to focus the attention of the nursing staff on this problem; secondly, it helped give medical staff guidance as to the level of pain, indicating the appropriate strength of analgesic; and thirdly, it helped Mr D. to feel that his pain was being noted and responded to (thus helping to reduce any feelings of anxiety and helplessness which may act as potentiators of perception of pain).

The only limitation of the pain assessment format is that when patients are in extreme pain it is difficult for them to concentrate on anything other than their pain, and indeed it was noticeably difficult for Mr D. to evaluate his pain properly because he was so absorbed and overwhelmed by the pain.

REFERENCE

Le Resche L (1982) Facial behaviour in pain: a study of candid photographs. *Journal of Non-Verbal Behaviour* 7: 46.

Care Study 3   Sleep, anxiety and pain
Summary by Morva Fordham

The experience of Mrs C. illustrates the interconnections of pain, sleep and anxiety. This woman in early middle age had undiagnosed pain. The pain occurred whenever she turned on her left side. She had consequently awakened at least three times per night for the past 4 months. On admission to hospital her sleep worsened due to the ward light and noise, to nocturia and acute anxiety about her unknown diagnosis. She complained of feeling sleepy all day, was loath to get up and wash, her legs felt weak and wobbly and her eyes heavy.

Three days after admission it was decided to review and alter her analgesics, the results of investigations were explained, she was given the opportunity to sleep during the day and had the curtains drawn around her bed at night.

Two days later Mrs C. was a new woman. She had been pain-free for two nights and had slept well. She only got up to pass urine and slept again quickly afterwards. She had been told the source of her pain—a renal tumour. She was washed, dressed, and made-up and stated that she felt well enough to go to work. This patient still had nocturia, (partially resulting from a high fluid intake), but her pain was relieved by analgesics though the source of her pain had not been eliminated. The care she received for pain, anxiety and sleep enabled her to face surgery in good heart.

Index